Vaughan Williams

Advisor in Music to Northeastern University Press

GUNTHER SCHULLER

Vaughan Williams

SIMON HEFFER

Northeastern University Press

BOSTON

Published in 2000 in England by Weidenfeld & Nicolson, London.
Published in 2001 in the United States of America by
Northeastern University Press, by arrangement
with Weidenfeld & Nicolson, a division of
The Orion Publishing Group
Limited, London.

Library of Congress Cataloging-in-Publication Data
Heffer, Simon.
Vaughan Williams / Simon Heffer.
p. cm.
Includes bibliographical references (p.) and discography (p.).
ISBN 1-55553-472-4 (cl.)
1. Vaughan Williams, Ralph, 1872–1958. 2. Composers—
England—Biography. I. Title.
ML410.V3 H37 2001
780´.92—dc21
[B]   00-052725

MANUFACTURED IN GREAT BRITAIN
05   04   03   02   01   5   4   3   2   1

To Michael Kennedy
'without permission'

Contents

Introduction

The image we have been left of Ralph Vaughan Williams could only be of an Englishman. He is middle-aged or elderly – as when he wrote his finest music – and everything about him is heavy: his frame, the tweeds that clothe it (he was once described as 'dressed as for stalking the folksong to its home'), and the look of thoughtful reserve on his face. If in our picture of him he is very old he is crowned with a shock of thick hair of purest white, though his face, like an infant's, is unlined, and his eyes are of a pale but penetrating grey. There is something stark, but at the same time deeply benevolent, about a man who (as his friend and biographer Michael Kennedy put it) set out deliberately to turn himself into an English composer. There were, of course, composers before him who were English by birth and upbringing – and there had been, on and off, for centuries. Of late, however, such men had written music whose inspiration was almost entirely German. What there had not been were composers who set out deliberately to write something that could be defined as English music, and which was not beholden to the Teutonic influence. That is why Vaughan Williams was important: he, with his contemporary and friend Gustav Holst, decided to manufacture a distinctly English musical voice, as no one had done in modern times, and take English music back to its roots.

Throughout his career, and after his death, Vaughan Williams risked paying the price of insularity for his daring. Yet now, over forty years since his death, his work is widely appreciated abroad, in America as well as in Europe, as it was in his lifetime. He is challenging Elgar's hitherto unquestioned supremacy as the leading composer of the English musical renaissance. Several recorded cycles of his nine symphonies are extant or in progress; his choral music, long dismissed as parochial and the province of amateur choirs, has undergone a revival and is now almost all available again on disc. Having suffered that traditional period of neglect that comes with the death of most composers, his music has steadily risen again, championed not least by conductors and musicians from outside the English tradition.

That Vaughan Williams became a composer was the result of a happy conjunction of inheritance and time. The affluence of his family, and an intellectualism inherited from both sides, allowed him to pursue a vocation that would make him no serious money until he was well into middle age. He also grew up at a time when there was a new national enthusiasm for music, led by men of will and determination who were prepared to make whatever personal sacrifice was necessary to further the cause. With his sense of *noblesse oblige* and his educated vision, Vaughan Williams was a kindred spirit of these men. He would come to write music that could legitimately be considered to be the work of a genius, but only after much slogging: but then this was a man who, in a proper English style, defined genius as 'the right man in the right place at the right time'.

He would become a symbol – in the view of many, the ultimate symbol – of the great renaissance in English music that can be dated from the opening of the Royal College of Music in London in 1883; and it was his good fortune to have the gifts and determination to compose in a self-created English style at a time when there was both a demand for and an encouragement of such a thing in his own country. He was fortunate that the founding fathers of the English musical renaissance, such as Sir Charles Hubert Parry, Sir Charles Villiers Stanford and Sir George Grove – all associated with the RCM from its foundation – were making a serious English musical life possible through their teaching and inspiration, and were both consciously and unconsciously creating an English school. Scarcely less important, the activities of such men had, for the first time, made music seem a fit career for a gentleman.

ONE

The Magic Casements

Vaughan Williams was born, as he put it in his old age, 'with a very small silver spoon in my mouth'. His father's family, which had come out of Carmarthenshire in the late eighteenth century, had made a reputation in the law. His mother was a Miss Wedgwood, niece of Charles Darwin. The family into which Ralph was born, on 12 October 1872, was of the highest professional class, one rank below the landed gentry. On both sides intellectualism and the peculiarly English brand of conservative radicalism that in those days so often accompanied it were strong forces. Arthur Vaughan Williams, Ralph's father, had chosen the church rather than the law. At his son's birth he was the vicar of Down Ampney, in Gloucestershire near the border with Wiltshire.

Music was one of the few intellectual disciplines into which one or other of Ralph's forebears had as yet made no serious incursion. The nineteenth century had, however, seen and heard new stirrings of the nation's musical consciousness. The pianoforte was the staple of domestic entertainment in many households. For over half a century choral societies had been springing up in provincial towns and cities, their

4

members devoted to performing the oratorios of Handel and Mendelssohn. Orchestral concerts had slowly come into fashion, their programmes similarly paying homage to the German masters. What passed for the English composer at the time of Vaughan Williams's birth were men who, with the honourable exception of Arthur Sullivan, slavishly devoted themselves to the Teutonic school, with Brahms and Wagner especially in vogue. There was, as yet, no English voice.

The increasingly musical climate of the mid to late Victorian period was the perfect stimulus for young Ralph. Music excited him from his earliest exposure to it in the family's drawing-room. He did not just want to sing it and play it: he wanted to write it. His first, rudimentary exercises in composition came in early childhood, though he showed none of the precocious genius of a Mozart or, even, of his successor Benjamin Britten. Learning how to write music would not come wholly instinctively. It would be the result of years of painstaking study, but would in time reveal a genius of musical invention. Vaughan Williams's musical apprenticeship would help create an artist who could connect English music with a cultural heritage that owed nothing to Germany, thereby relating it more easily to many of the English people. He would, by the end of his life, have established the English voice.

When Ralph was two and a half his father died suddenly, aged just forty. His mother took him and her other two children back to Leith Hill Place, the Wedgwood home, in perhaps the most beautiful part of the Surrey hills between Guildford and Dorking. His was a serene, comfortable childhood, though his creative motivation had no complacency about it. The Wedgwoods had, like many such households of the time, a strong musical element in the home. His aunt Sophy Wedgwood taught Ralph the piano. It was for this instrument that he wrote his first composition, at the age of six: a four-bar piece called *The Robin's Nest*. She also worked with him through a Georgian textbook called *A Child's Introduction to Thorough Bass*. At the age of seven he began violin lessons, his mother having by chance seen an advertisement by a teacher while walking with her son through Eastbourne. The following year he tackled Stainer's *Harmony*, and took an Edinburgh University correspondence course. Music was barely taught in schools then, and all this extra-curricular activity meant that by the time Ralph went to his preparatory school, at Rottingdean in the autumn of 1883, he was more than equal to whatever musical instruction could be thrown at him. The climax of his career at that school, he felt, was playing Raff's *Cavatina* in a school concert. It was also at Rottingdean that an enlightened piano teacher introduced him properly to Bach (young Ralph had hitherto thought no one a match for Handel), thereby increasing his interest in the piano and beginning a lifelong love affair with the man who would become his favourite composer.

When he arrived at Charterhouse in January 1887, at the age of fourteen, he was used to arranging chamber music for whatever instrumental forces happened to be available. Charterhouse encouraged musical expression, which made it progressive among the public schools of its time. The school organist, H. G. Robinson, let Ralph practise on the chapel organ. There was a school orchestra in which he played the violin and then the viola, which would become a favourite instrument. The Charterhouse music-makers were sufficiently ambitious that Ralph and a colleague asked the formidable headmaster, Haig Brown, whether they could give a concert in the school hall. To their surprise he assented, and the occasion was attended by masters as well as boys. Vaughan Williams recalled that, afterwards, a mathematics master came up to him and said: 'You must go on.' It was, the composer also noted, 'one of the few words of encouragement I have ever received'. At this stage he was, however, so convinced of his own vocation to write music that he needed no encouragement.

By the time he left Charterhouse in 1890 Vaughan Williams had become an atheist. That state of mind continued throughout his student days, though he later moderated his view to agnosticism. As his second wife put it: 'He was far too deeply absorbed by music to feel any need of religious observance.' He never became a professing Christian. He was all too susceptible, however, to the aesthetic beauty of Anglican ritual, of the Prayer Book, the King James Bible and church music. His recognition of its quality was part of his instinctive sympathy with the culture of England, its apparently inevitable power over him driving him in his own particular direction when he reached maturity as a composer. Despite his atheism he was a deeply humane figure, bred with a strong sense of *noblesse oblige*, and also harbouring a deep sentimentality towards his environment, landscape and fellow countrymen. All these qualities would manifest themselves in his music.

In the autumn of 1890 he took the first crucial step in his career, and enrolled at the Royal College of Music. The College had been founded only seven years earlier by Sir George Grove, who was still director. Largely as a result of its existence, musical life in England was in a new and exciting phase, and pioneers were still needed. Vaughan Williams's immediate ambition had been to become an orchestral player, probably of the viola; but this was unthinkable to his family, who regarded such an occupation as *infra dignitatem*. They would only countenance his becoming an organist, which at least smacked of respectability. By the time he went to the RCM he had not only become used to practising on the Charterhouse organ, but would also out of term make a daily pilgrimage from Leith Hill to the church at nearby Coldharbour, and practise there. Once at the RCM, though, his ambitions developed: he wanted to study composition, and to do so under Parry. He achieved his ambition, thereby coming under one of the most important influences he would know.

Parry can properly be seen, now, as one of the most vital and radical forces of the English musical renaissance. The son and heir of a Gloucestershire squire and aesthete, he had much in common socially and intellectually with his new pupil. Above all, both brought to their vocation a capacity to think originally about it. Parry had become celebrated first as a writer nearly a decade earlier, with his *Studies of Great Composers*. His reputation as a composer had been properly established in 1887 by his great choral work *Blest Pair of Sirens*, a setting of Milton, which Vaughan Williams maintained (Elgar, Byrd and Purcell notwithstanding) was his favourite piece of choral music written by an Englishman. Although easily labelled as a Germanicist, and with a heavy and freely acknowledged debt to Brahms, Parry none the less led the movement to free English music of its German subservience. Before he and his pupil had met, Parry's music had had its effect on Vaughan Williams, or at least on his instincts. In his *Musical Autobiography* Vaughan Williams wrote: 'I remember, even as a boy, my brother saying to me that there was something, to his mind, peculiarly English about his music.' Long before Vaughan Williams developed the notion that music could be national, and that England, too, had a 'national music', he instinctively knew there were idioms of atavistic English music, whether of Tudor polyphony or of folk-song, that bore a cultural fingerprint peculiar to his homeland. He heard this in Parry too, and would devote much of the first phase of his maturity as a composer to finding, and defining, it.

Before being allowed into Parry's orbit, the potential pupil had to reach an advanced standard in harmony, which Vaughan Williams duly did. Once qualified to study with Parry, he found a well of humanity and conviction remarkably similar to his own. Parry recognised in his pupil a gifted amateur like himself who also had the drive to pursue music to the highest professional standard. He looked for talent and 'character' in compositions that Vaughan Williams himself later came to recognise as deeply sub-standard. He embarked on educating his pupil more widely about music, a harder task in an era before gramophone records and broadcasting, playing through works on the piano and lending him scores which – if orchestral – he and a fellow pupil would play through as a duet on the piano, in order to discover the works from the inside.

Parry tried to educate his pupil about Beethoven, whose idiom repelled him – and continued to do so – though Vaughan Williams admitted that Parry had made him see Beethoven's greatness none the less. Above all, Parry made him realise he stood in a tradition of English composition that had begun with William Byrd, however rickety it might have become since the death of Purcell two hundred years earlier. He once told his pupil to 'write choral music as befits an Englishman and a democrat'. It was advice Vaughan Williams would heed, though when he left the RCM for Trinity College, Cambridge, in October 1892, the most profound influence upon him, he felt, was Wagner.

His experience with Wagner exemplified the romantic side of his character, and also the way in which inspiration came to him, and how his art would consist in expressing deep-seated cultural instincts within him. Between leaving Charterhouse and going to the RCM he had had his first taste of Wagner opera, *Die Walküre*. On hearing it he experienced 'that strange certainty that I had heard it all before. There was a feeling of recognition as of meeting an old friend which comes to us all in the face of all artistic experiences. I had the same experience when I first heard an English folk-song, when I first saw Michael Angelo's *Day and Night*, when I suddenly came upon Stonehenge, or had my first sight of New York City – the intimation that I had been there already.' As well as this almost supernatural element to his appreciation of art, Vaughan Williams was drawn to music by its mystical function – which it is easy to label as a substitute for religion – and, perhaps for the same reason, to its uses as a vehicle for prophecy, or at least for making quasi-prophetic utterances. This feature of his art would come through most strongly in his later years; it is in works such as his anti-war cantata *Dona Nobis Pacem*, or in the stunning Sixth Symphony, when he seems (though he strenuously denied it) to see the world after a nuclear apocalypse. In great old age, having written both those works, he told an audience of schoolchildren: 'Music will enable you to see past facts to the very essence of things in a way which science cannot do. The arts are the means by which we can look through the magic casements and see what lies behind.'

He read history at Cambridge, because the programme of lectures did not conflict with the days he wished to return to London to study with Parry. At Cambridge he had lessons with Charles Wood for the degree of Bachelor of Music, and took further instruction on the organ. Cambridge developed his intellectual life, not least through his family connections: the place was dotted with Darwins and Wedgwoods, and he came to know the family of Frederic Maitland, the Master of Downing College, whose father-in-law Herbert Fisher had been at Oxford with Arthur Vaughan Williams. He also befriended George Trevelyan, who in time would become a distinguished historian, and the budding philosopher George Moore. The main characteristics of Vaughan Williams's intellectual life outside music – his love of the written word, his rather political sense of ideas, his philosophical earn-estness – were well established in these days.

This was the generation before Rupert Brooke, and the fashionable idealism of the Fabians that he came to embody.

However, having become part of this circle, Vaughan Williams also joined them in reading the Fabian tracts, and became what he defined as a socialist. He was never, though, ideological, seeming to prefer the pragmatism that united his class in the early twentieth century whether it was professed by a Tory, Socialist or Liberal. Although he would always take a keen interest in national and world affairs, his politics remained those of the typical, bloody-minded English radical. Writing in 1952, he told a fellow composer: 'I think that when I am with conservatives I become socialistic and when I am with socialists I become a true blue Tory.' Later on in his life, when he saw socialism transmuting, or mutating, into Stalin's variant of communism, he rejected the idea and dissociated himself from it. In the same 1952 letter he said that 'ever since I had a vote I have voted either Radical or Labour except once, after the last war when I was so disgusted by what I considered the mean trick of the Labour party in forcing an election. I voted Labour in the last election [1951] though in my heart of hearts I wanted the Tories to get in, but the old spirit of opposition crept up and with all the country shouting for the Tories I determined to be on the other side.' He would not be the only socialist to recant once he actually saw the ideal put into practice, both at home and abroad, and noted how it militated against both freedom and prosperity. Mr Kennedy has perceptively analysed these traits in saying that Vaughan Williams 'had a great sense of the artist's part in the community – almost a communist (idealist communist) outlook but with a big streak of personal obstinacy . . . he didn't like commissions or writing to order.'

Cambridge in the eighteen nineties had a good musical life. Vaughan Williams was an active participant in the university's Musical Club, at which, one Saturday evening, he heard the first public performance of one of his own works, a quartet for men's voices. He took his BMus in 1894, and a second in history the following year; and then he had to consider in detail his likely career. Alan Gray, who had been teaching him the organ at Cambridge, confided in his fellow organ-tutor at the RCM that he could not in all conscience advise Vaughan Williams to make a career as an organist because he was 'so hopelessly unhandy'. He rejoined the RCM in the summer of 1895, and had another of the crucial encounters that was to affect his musical style and outlook: he met Gustav von Holst, as he was then known, a man who Vaughan Williams later said was 'the greatest influence on my music'.

Von Holst was two years his new friend's junior. His was a family of professional musicians who had come to Britain from Riga, though they were of Swedish origins. He had already some experience as a freelance orchestral player, but none of the social ease or confidence of Vaughan Williams. Despite Vaughan Williams's own well-formed intellectual life, von Holst from the start had more original lines of thought, having a particular interest in the culture and mysticism of the Orient. He had a less romantic vision of England, and a pessimism and sense of isolation that caused some to think his music lacked warmth. Much of it did: but the realism, freedom from sentiment and absence of cliché this lent it are partly what has caused his music to endure, and to make it seem so innovative, even now. Adrian Boult, who knew them both well, recognised that Vaughan Williams lacked the gift of scoring that Holst (he dropped the 'von' during the Great War, in response to anti-German feeling at the time) possessed in abundance: learning how to orchestrate would occupy Vaughan Williams greatly until he was in his late thirties, and unquestionably retarded his progress as a composer.

He and Holst soon began to have 'field days', on which they would spend several hours deconstructing each other's compositions. 'I think he showed all he wrote to me and I nearly all I wrote to him,' Vaughan Williams recalled. 'I say "nearly all" advisedly, because sometimes I could not face the absolute integrity of his vision and I hid some of my worst crimes from him.' This mutual soul-baring, a manifestation of the complete honesty and (to use his own word) integrity of Vaughan Williams's character, made for a close and unshakeable intimacy, and one that would last forty years until Holst's death. In 1903 Holst wrote to him from Germany, in response to some worrying that Vaughan Williams was doing about his own abilities, to say that 'you have never lost your invention but it has not developed enough. Your best – your most original and beautiful style or "atmosphere" is an indescribable sort of feeling as if one was listening to very lovely lyrical poetry. I may be wrong but I think this (what I call to myself the *real* RVW) is more original than you think.' He added, as a word of warning: 'when you are not in this strain, you either write "second class goods" or you have a devil of a bother to write anything at all'.

Holst was instinctively the better and more disciplined

musician, and Vaughan Williams learned immensely from him. He repaid him with his own musical influence, but also more practically: Holst and his wife were often short of money, and Vaughan Williams would help them to afford much-needed holidays, and even subsidised concerts in the early years of their careers to ensure that his friend's music – and his – were performed. Throughout his life Vaughan Williams's philanthropy would never be simply theoretical, and his generosity – both material and of his spirit – remained instinctive and apparently inexhaustible.

In terms of his musical development, the great difference between Vaughan Williams's second spell at the RCM and his first was that the sway of Wagner had been replaced by an addiction to the supposedly redundant modal form of early English and European music. The modes had been the original grammar of music, as invented by the Greeks. They would now, with great unconventionalism, dominate Vaughan Williams's attempts at composition. Unlike the scales that largely replaced them, the modes did not have a key; as the *Oxford Companion to Music* defines it:

All our major keys are, except for pitch, precisely alike; a listener with an excellent ear cannot tell one from another unless he happens to possess the gift of 'absolute pitch'. The difference between one mode and another is not the kind of difference which exists between C major and D major but that which exists between C major and C minor or D major and D minor, i.e. a difference of the arrangement of tones and semitones, and hence, necessarily, of the width of some of the other intervals. It may be called a difference of *flavour* . . .

Vaughan Williams had found this form of music in Tudor polyphony, and especially in madrigals of the period. It was also detectable in some of the supposedly unsophisticated English folk-songs of which he was becoming increasingly aware; and the 'flavour' appealed to him because it seemed to be peculiarly English. He might have been able to explore the modes, and their potential when applied to contemporary composition, in an original way with a broad-minded teacher like Parry; but Parry had now become director of the RCM, and Vaughan Williams studied instead with Charles Villiers Stanford, a mercurial and plain-spoken Irishman. In his *Musical Autobiography*, the pupil admitted Stanford was 'a great teacher, but I believe I was unteachable'. The more he thought about the use of modes in composition, the more he realised that he wished to go in that direction, rather than follow more modern compositional practices. While a supremely gifted radical like Parry might have indulged him, the more rigid Stanford was unsympathetic. He had no great liking for his pupil's music, which he considered 'ugly'.

For all his difficulties with Stanford, by the time Vaughan Williams finally left the RCM in 1897 he was a fully paid-up member of the English musical establishment that had, in barely fifteen years, been created around the College; and there he would stay, and eventually become its leader. For all the radicalism of his politics, and for all his subsequent attempts to found a national school of English music, he was destined to be deeply affected by the natural conservatism of the RCM's approach to composition. Above all, he was determined to explode what he called the 'cigar theory' of music: that it was a luxury which, like cigars, could not be made at home, but had to be imported.

The eighteen nineties were a time when the generation of composers above Vaughan Williams started, by their deeds rather than their words, to prove the point for him. His teacher, Hubert Parry, was increasingly showing that he was not merely a bespoke manufacturer of high Victorian oratorios. His *Lady Radnor Suite* of 1894 evokes exuberance as well as gentility, exhibiting none of the stodginess of the German tradition in which it was accepted Parry was steeped, and from which he could not, it was believed, escape. More significantly, his *Symphonic Variations* of 1897 demonstrate a passion, suavity and coherence that Vaughan Williams would not come close to emulating until the *London Symphony* more than fifteen years later. That the *Variations* have stayed in the repertoire, and have enjoyed new popularity and appreciation in our own times by conductors from all over the world is a tribute to the originality and power of Parry's work. Most significant of all – because it had a technical brilliance, inventive genius and popular success that truly put contemporary English music on the map – was the arrival, in 1899, of Edward Elgar's *Enigma Variations*.

It would be some years yet before Vaughan Williams's own work could rival the fame or the reach of such music. He had to content himself, for the present, with humbler activities. For all his apparent inability with the instrument – not to mention his atheism – he soon found a post as organist at the church of St Barnabas in South Lambeth, then as now one of the poorer districts of London. He had an advantage over other aspiring composers such as Holst in that he did not need to earn a living, having a healthy but not excessive private income. His work as an organist was for his continuing education, not to keep body and soul together. He used the post as a springboard for other musical activities. As well as training the choir for their duties during services he founded a choral society and an orchestral society – 'both of them pretty bad' – which made him realise more acutely the practicalities of writing music for performance. His time at St Barnabas was not easy. He told Holst that his choristers were 'louts' and the vicar 'quite mad'. However, it instilled in him a proper understanding of what had to be done if a piece of music intended for performance by amateurs as well as professionals was to have a chance of success; though this, in turn, would lead to the criticism later on in his career that his choral music in particular retained, in the pejorative sense, an amateur tinge, and was unsuited to professional performances in the great concert halls.

Despite his relegation in Vaughan Williams's estimation, Wagner had still not yet been properly put in perspective by the young composer. He made his first big European journey in 1897 not to Italy, as Stanford had advised him so that he could hear the native opera at La Scala and rid himself of the influence of the Teuton, but to Berlin, which was the only city in Europe where one could hear *The Ring* uncut. The trip was also his honeymoon; on 9 October 1897, three days before his twenty-fifth birthday, he married Adeline Fisher, sister-in-law of Frederic Maitland and daughter of his father's friend Herbert Fisher. The pair had met frequently at Cambridge while Vaughan Williams had been an undergraduate, and had many intellectual, as well as musical, interests in common.

With the exception of a visit to Italy at Christmas 1897, the Vaughan Williamses spent six months in Berlin. Through mutual friends Vaughan Williams managed to arrange to take lessons from Max Bruch, professor of composition at the Hochschule für Musik. What he found so valuable in Bruch was the way in which he encouraged his pupil – 'I had never had much encouragement before.' When a teacher himself, Vaughan Williams made a point of urging on his own pupils, for 'I would rather be guilty of encouraging a fool than of discouraging a genius'. He returned to London, and to his post in South Lambeth, and his musical life consisted more of performing and listening than of composing, despite Bruch's influence. Aware that for all his dedication and skill he was not the most natural of composers, and certainly no prodigy, Vaughan Williams was guilty of allowing a lack of professional self-confidence to overwhelm his otherwise considerable talents; but he was, still, waiting for the right spark to come along and ignite his creativity.

A new incumbent at St Barnabas's insisted on the organist taking communion, which Vaughan Williams felt he, as a principled atheist, could not; so he resigned, without any apparent regret, early in 1899. As a result, he had more time for composition, writing in the first instance his *Heroic Elegy* for orchestra. This was performed at the RCM in March 1901 to some acclaim from, among others, Stanford. Sadly, it was not published. He was also writing criticism for musical journals – he was at this stage more a scholar and musicologist than anything else – and had yet, as he neared the age of thirty, to write any music that made a great public impact. He proceeded to the degree of Doctor of Music at Cambridge, and so gloried in his academic title that he refused to exchange it for any other, such as a knighthood, for the rest of his life; he was always from then on 'Dr Vaughan Williams'.

The acquisition of his doctorate led to his writing about music and lecturing upon it with increasing frequency. Composing remained, however, his prime ambition, and at last the pressure to compose helped overcome the obstacles of professional self-confidence that he had imposed upon himself. He summoned up the courage to write to Elgar, still in the first flush of his great fame, to ask whether he could become a pupil for the purposes of learning about orchestration. Mrs Elgar politely replied that her husband was too busy to take on pupils, and suggested Vaughan Williams went to Granville Bantock instead. Bantock was then principal of the music school of the Midland Institute at Birmingham. Vaughan Williams ignored Elgar's suggestion – something he later admitted he regretted. Instead, he sought to learn from Elgar vicariously, by sitting in the British Museum for hours on end studying the scores of the *Enigma Variations* and the *Dream of Gerontius*: from which he claimed he gained much, as he said was apparent from his *Sea Symphony* of 1910. His problem, and one that he never really shook off – according to Roy Douglas, a composer who helped him prepare his scores in later life – was that he could always imagine exactly what sound he wished to create, but could not always easily determine how to have the orchestra make that sound. This was something that Holst had no difficulty in doing; and, moreover, Holst scored his music in a way that ensured every instrument told, whereas Vaughan Williams's orchestral writing sometimes led to a thickness of sound that ended up obscuring some of what he had written.

Vaughan Williams's first popular piece, which started to make his name as a composer, was not orchestral but vocal: his setting of the poem 'Linden Lea', by William Barnes. Michael Kennedy has categorised *Linden Lea* as 'midway between a folk song and an art song', a description hard to improve upon. It sounds like an English song that has been around for ever; but in writing the music Vaughan Williams revealed once more his instinctive Englishness, mimicking a version of national folk-song before he had embarked upon his heroic task of collecting them. The song caused a minor sensation; it was on a level of sophistication and subtlety well above many of the drawing-room ballads, with their excessive sentimentality and histrionics, that were the staple of the recreational singers to be found in almost every family. Suddenly, Vaughan Williams found he had made a reputation as a writer of songs, and was in demand as such: and he quickly followed up this initial success with the publication of other songs written in the preceding years. One work from his bottom drawer was a setting of poems by Dante Gabriel Rossetti, *The House of Life*, which included what would become one of his most celebrated songs, *Silent Noon*. He had been working, too, on a cycle of Robert Louis Stevenson's *Songs of Travel*, whose alternating qualities of robustness and sensitivity won them lasting popularity. It was through songs such as these that, as he passed the age of thirty, he became properly noticed on the English musical scene.

Two

Real Music

As well as writing about his musical ideas, Vaughan Williams devoted more and more time to his evangelising work as a lecturer. He concentrated in his lectures on the question of whether or not music could be 'national'; whether there was, or could be, a distinctive English voice. During a series of lectures at Bournemouth in the winter of 1901–2 he contrasted Germany, where public funding helped provide orchestras for almost every decent-sized town, with England, where musical education and public music making were, despite the advances of recent years, still the province of a struggling minority. With few orchestras, and few conductors – especially outside London – willing to promote new music from home, composition was often an act of futility. Before there could be a national music – and Vaughan Williams believed the phenomenon was latent and waiting to be awakened – there had to be the means of making that music. 'What we want in England', he wrote in *The Vocalist* in 1902, 'is *real* music, even if it be only a music-hall song. Provided it possess real feeling and real life, it will be worth all the off scourings of the classics in the world.'

The national music had its roots, he knew, in folk-song. He lectured on the subject all over England, using material already generally available; but the songs everyone knew were but a fraction of those in existence. Since 1898 there had been a Folk-Song Society, which had included Parry and Stanford among its vice-presidents, whose existence was more the result of the rising musical consciousness in England than due to any great desire to reintroduce these fine old tunes to the English people – that would come later, in an almost militant way. In December 1903 Vaughan Williams was giving one of his lectures at Brentwood in Essex, after which it was suggested to him that he attend a parish tea being given in the adjacent village of Ingrave for the local elderly. One such, a labourer called Mr Potiphar, told the composer that if he returned the next day he would sing him some old songs that he might not know.

So, on 4 December 1903 he collected, from Potiphar, his first folk-song, the haunting *Bushes and Briars*. This was the spark that ignited his creativity; on hearing it Vaughan Williams had a moment of revelation, connected as much with instinct and sentiment as with any function of the intellect. The song has a quality Vaughan Williams had also identified in *Dives and Lazarus*, a tune he had first come across in 1893 and which he used as the basis of one of his most enduring orchestral pieces forty years later: that, on first hearing the tune, it strikes the listener as though he has known it all his life. It has that strain of heroic melancholy and profound peace that is religiose without being religious; it is an evocation of the ancient rhythms of the English countryside and English life, stripped of sentiment and romanticism. It echoes and represents the mysticism that would become a dominant strain in Vaughan Williams's character, a substitute for orthodox religion that would increasingly inform his music.

This discovery turned Vaughan Williams's already active interest in folk-song into an obsession. It also altered, fundamentally, the entire direction of his music, and helped him to a new style in which he discovered a greater coherence and naturalness than he had felt before. He began to tour the countryside with a notebook, accosting elderly artisans and jotting down whatever tunes they could sing to him. Just as Wagner had obsessed him in his teens, and the modes in his twenties, so this new influence came to dominate him now. Speaking in 1932 of the discovery, he said that 'several of us found here in its simplest form the musical idiom which we unconsciously were cultivating in ourselves, it gave a point to our imagination; far from fettering us, it freed us from foreign influences which weighed on us, which we could not get rid of, but which we felt were not pointing in the direction in which we really wanted to go'.

The effects would be spectacularly far-reaching: folk-songs would not merely shape Vaughan Williams as a composer, they would, through him, shape a whole school of English music that would for years be indissolubly associated with the Royal College and what would come to be called the 'English musical establishment'. Holst was Vaughan Williams's main associate and accomplice in this project; later they would be joined by a younger man, George Butterworth. Parry, who shared their interests, looked upon it all benevolently, but was too old a dog to learn such new tricks, and was in any case pursuing a mood of greater introversion and reflectiveness in what would become his later orchestral works. Uninfluenced by folk-song, indebted to the German romantic mainstream and a genius *sui generis*, Elgar remained above, or beyond, this new obsession. When asked what he thought of the vogue for folk-music, he simply replied: 'I am folk-music.' It was consistent with the high esteem he had for himself after years of failure, self-doubt and unfulfilment of his spectacular talent. On another occasion, when asked by a young Frenchman whether he could, as an aspiring composer himself, write to Elgar, Elgar assented. When asked where he should write, Sir Edward replied: 'England is address enough for me.'

Yet for all his stated resistance to the 'national music', Elgar was, Vaughan Williams felt, as susceptible as anyone else to the newly prevailing wind: his younger colleague thought that he detected in the fifth of the *Enigma Variations* ('RPA') 'the same sense of familiarity, the same sense of the something peculiarly belonging to me as an Englishman which I also felt when I heard "Bushes and Briars" or "Lazarus" '. The variation, dedicated to Matthew Arnold's son Richard, a gifted amateur musician, certainly has by turns the melancholy, reflectiveness, nobility and humour that are so frequently the components of the best English folk tunes, and no discernible Brahmsian heaviness. Just as Vaughan Williams made a conscious decision to take his idiom from the people (albeit a romanticised, atavistic people), Elgar appears to have made a conscious decision to write the theme-music of Empire, of Edwardian grandeur, of a society of prosperity, certainty and (occasionally) pomp and

25

circumstance. However different their outlooks – and Vaughan Williams was never the conservative man that his older colleague revelled in being – they were both subject to the influences of the same environment, the same culture, the same nation.

Similarly, Vaughan Williams felt that younger composers who in later years rebelled against the new orthodoxy he had created none the less owed something to it. In his own lectures on 'National Music' of 1932, he said that 'I know in my own mind that if it had not been for the folk-song movement of twenty-five years ago this young and vital school represented by such names as [William] Walton, [Arthur] Bliss, [Constant] Lambert, and Patrick Hadley would not have come into being. They may deny their own birthright; but having once drunk deep of the living water no amount of Negroid emetics or "Baroque" purgatives will enable them to expel it from their system.' He also pointed out, with reference to such as Chopin, Smetana, Wagner and Rimsky-Korsakov that there were precedents for nationalism in music before the English variety was founded. As for Stravinsky, who seems to have represented the ultimate in anti-nationalism to Vaughan Williams (though he admired some of his music), he was 'too intent on shocking the bourgeois to have time to think about making his own people "feel at home".' Referring to experiments with various influences that Stravinsky had conducted – and with scant sympathy for his life as an exile after the Russian Revolution, which of necessity dislocated him from his roots – Vaughan Williams comments that this was 'not the work of a serious composer, but rather that of the too clever

26

craftsman, one might almost say, the feats of the precocious child.'

For all his criticism of Stravinsky for experimenting with, among other things, the 'Negroid emetic' of jazz – and the comment at the conclusion of his 1932 lectures that jazz (some of which he liked) was an art indigenous to America that sat ill in the works of a few French and German contemporary composers who made the 'pitiful effort' to 'add a little sting to their failing inventiveness by adopting a few jazz rhythms' – he, too, would eventually come under this influence. There were distant sounds of it in the next of his major works to be unveiled after this series of lectures, his Piano Concerto in C, first performed in 1933; in 1936 he would set the poems of John Skelton in *Five Tudor Portraits* because their rhythms were, as Elgar had told him, 'pure jazz'; he would pay homage to Henry Hall, the leader of the BBC Dance Orchestra, in his *Partita for Double String Orchestra*; and his great Sixth Symphony, shot through with jazz rhythms, would pay the most glaring tribute of all to the new music by featuring a solo saxophonist in its scherzo.

Back in Edwardian England, as he sought to propel his own career forward, Vaughan Williams was putting his energies more and more into writing occasional orchestral pieces. One such was the *Symphonic Rhapsody*, given by Dan Godfrey at Bournemouth in March 1904; but, slowly and subtly, the new influences and inspirations to which he was now subject led to a more ambitious idea, a vehicle in which he could properly and expansively celebrate them. He had determined to write a symphony. Showing that, of all the influences that had come upon him during his musical apprenticeship, that of Parry was at this stage the foremost, it was to be a choral symphony on a grand scale. At its conception in late 1903, the working title for it was *The Ocean*. It would be seven years before its first performance, by which stage it had become *A Sea Symphony*. It took so long to execute not so much because of lack of confidence on the part of the composer, but because of his mounting workload. Cecil Sharp, his fellow folk-song collector and the man who helped confirm Vaughan Williams's belief in the central importance of folk-song to English music, had recommended him – as a former church organist – to the Revd Percy Dearmer, one of a group of clerics so dissatisfied with the new *Hymns Ancient and Modern* that they determined to commission a new hymn book, which became *The English Hymnal*.

Vaughan Williams, his agnosticism (as it had now become) notwithstanding, agreed to Dearmer's proposal. As well as rounding up fine hymn tunes that *Ancient and Modern* had missed, the composer found that many of the folk-songs he was turning up in his other work perfectly fitted words that had no known music. Occasionally, he would find tunes he felt deserved to be hymns, and had Dearmer or one of his clerical friends supply words for them. Where no music could be found to suit some fine words, Vaughan Williams himself would write some under the label 'anon'. This was how his most famous hymn tune, *Sine Nomine*, came about, to fit the words of 'For all the Saints'. The result, when the Hymnal was published in 1906, was to plug Vaughan Williams directly into what, in that less secular age, was still one of the main currents of English culture.

In the two years he spent on this project, he worried whether he was not in fact ossifying as a composer himself, since he had so little time for original composition of his own. He soon realised, however, that this 'close association with some of the best (as well as some of the worst) tunes in the world was a better musical education than any amount of sonatas and fugues'. However, he was able to use the church as a medium for the promulgation of the ethos of the national school of music that he was setting about creating: the music in the *Hymnal* is steeped in polyphony and folk-song, a radical departure for the times but one that reconnected the church, and the millions who attended it, with 'old England' by way of the new musical life of the country. It was perhaps just as well that, in seeking to do this, his mind was unclouded by any thoughts or scruples of religion. For him this was a project of cultural, not religious, evangelism.

He had work in other respects that brought him closer to the makers of music, the people whom Parry had praised as 'we singing English'. Others in the Surrey hills formed a committee in 1904 to establish a musical event in Dorking, to be known as the Leith Hill Festival, the purpose of which was as much to provide opportunities for music-making, with competitions between choirs, as to give entertainment to those who wished to attend and listen. As a man who was fast acquiring a reputation in national musical circles, and whose family still lived locally, Vaughan Williams was high on the committee's list of those it intended to invite to participate. His missionary beliefs in music-making would never have allowed him to decline their invitation. Over the next fifty years he conducted choirs and orchestras, taught and wrote music for the festival. It was his most important and direct connection with the people who made music, and who were therefore the lifeblood of musical life in England. He never saw music in a vacuum, or as self-indulgent. Its practical purpose continued to motivate his work as long as he lived.

Despite such intensive labour, he continued to write other, more ambitious orchestral pieces, giving the lie to his reservations about the effect on his creativity of his work on the *Hymnal*. During 1904 he had worked on a 'symphonic impression', as he called it, *In the Fen Country*. He revised it twice before its first performance in 1909, and again in 1935; it was not published until after his death, since when it has been performed regularly and recorded several times. In its understatement and sombreness it reflects not just the landscape it was intended to, but also sounds in retrospect the most Holstian of Vaughan Williams's works. This, perhaps, reflects not only the closeness of their working relationship at the time, but also the fact that Holst had a clearer idea of and belief in his own idiom at the time than his friend did.

A tour of Norfolk in January 1905 led to some rich discoveries of folk-songs around King's Lynn, including three – *The Captain's Apprentice*, *The Bold Young Sailor* and *On Board a '98* – that became the constituent parts of the first *Norfolk Rhapsody*, one of the earliest orchestral works of Vaughan Williams's still to be in the repertoire, and which was first performed at the Queen's Hall in London in August 1906. As with *Bushes and Briars*, the overwhelming flavour of the songs – with the exception of *On Board a '98* – is melancholy, the hardships of life being to the fore in place of any of the presumed bucolic cheeriness of Olde England. Two of the mistaken pieces of received wisdom about Vaughan Williams are that his music is predominantly pastoral, and that this pastorality is inevitably idyllic. Neither is true. There were two other rhapsodies based on material from Norfolk, but both were withdrawn by the composer despite having several performances before the Great War. The manuscript of the second still exists, though with two pages missing; the manuscript of the third is lost. The composer had planned the three rhapsodies to form a Norfolk Symphony, but abandoned the idea.

As well as the inspiration he was deriving almost literally from the soil of England, Vaughan Williams was, like many in his generation, coming under the spell of the poetry of Walt Whitman. To refined palates nearly a century later the devotion with which this rather ordinary American poet was regarded by intelligent men and women is a cause of curiosity. Certainly, the words that Vaughan Williams used in *A Sea Symphony* do not inevitably make the listener appreciate fully the excellence of the music. While continuing to work on the symphony, Vaughan Williams planned another excursion into Whitman, with a setting for orchestra and chorus of *Toward the Unknown Region*, first performed in 1907. It sounds like a necessary expression of Vaughan Williams's mystical side, of a post-Christian union between art and nature. It is more remarkable for the way in which the music, often reminiscent of the dignity and restraint of Parry, acts as a precursor to the first truly mature works of a few years later, such as *On Wenlock Edge* and the *Tallis Fantasia*. Even since the contemporary *Norfolk Rhapsodies* the style has developed. While owing something to the idiom of folk-song, there is an originality and scope of invention that reflect more the earlier obsession with modality, but which come across as the first flowerings of the distinct voice of the composer.

Before the early great works could be completed, there was one more act of apprenticeship that Vaughan Williams had to undergo. He knew his great technical weakness as an orchestrator had still not been overcome – 'In 1908 I came to the conclusion that I was lumpy and stodgy' – and he contemplated going to France to study with the very un-lumpy and unstodgy Vincent d'Indy. 'I had come to a dead end,' he recalled in his *Musical Autobiography*, 'and a little French polish would be of use to me.' D'Indy, then in his late fifties, had been the pupil and disciple of César Franck, a composer for whom Vaughan Williams appears to have had an intemperate loathing. Instead, on the advice of a mutual friend, he went to study with Maurice Ravel, three years his junior, who was little known in England at that time and not an obvious choice. It was an inspired decision by Vaughan Williams. In France, Ravel was infamous for his composi-tional radicalism, which had upset the native musical estab-lishment, but which was helping to give French music an *avant-garde* reputation second to none in Europe at the time.

In his twenties, Ravel had experimented with oriental musical forms in the search for a new grammar of music, just as his new pupil had experimented with the modes. He had an almost disturbingly open mind. He quickly made Vaughan Williams see that the 'heavy contrapuntal Teutonic manner was not necessary', and a lightness comes into his pupil's music almost from then on – though the Teuton did reassert himself from time to time, leading to occasional moments of unsubtlety. 'He showed me', Vaughan Williams said, 'how to orchestrate in points of colour rather than in lines.' Ravel dismissed Brahms and Tchaikovsky, the two recently dead romantic masters, as 'tous les deux un peu lourds', and characterised his own music as 'tout à fait simple, rien que Mozart'.

This was the style Ravel's new pupil needed to emulate if he was to eliminate the thickness from his own writing. The Frenchman also offered Vaughan Williams an acute appraisal of Elgar, which served to highlight the differences between him and the man who would assume his mantle: he was 'tout à fait Mendelssohn'. For his part, the pupil felt that ten years with this brilliant innovator and technician would not teach him all he wanted to know. As well as introducing Vaughan Williams to the music of Borodin and Rimsky-Korsakov, Ravel also helped absolve him of the guilt of writing so much of his music on the piano, which the Englishman had considered marked him out as amateurish. 'Sans le piano on ne peut pas inventer des nouvelles harmonies,' he told him, and that was that.

Ravel's estimate of Elgar, while somewhat provocative, had a ring of accuracy about it. The link between oratorios such as *Gerontius* and Mendelssohn's output was straightforward to make; though in much of his other writing Elgar had brought to bear a lightness of touch and a bright originality not always apparent in the later nineteenth-century German masters from whom, also, some of his style seems to have been derived. What really distinguishes Vaughan Williams from him, however, is not that the younger man did not have the obligation to German music, but that he had one to the modes, Tudor polyphony and, finally, English folk-song. The works of Vaughan Williams's early maturity all scream out their differences from anything Elgar had written. While Vaughan Williams's songs were intensely influenced by folk-song, Elgar's owe more to *lieder* or, in the case of his orchestral songs (Op. 48, 59 and 60) the contemporary overt romanticism of a Verdi or Puccini. Had Vaughan Williams taken Stanford's advice and spent his six months' honeymoon in Milan, things might have been different, though the emotional complexity of much of Elgar's writing is not simply down to the continental influence, but betrays the fact that he was a far more complex and tortured character than Vaughan Williams.

While Elgar's *Introduction and Allegro* for strings is a vigorous, utterly modern piece, the *Fantasia on a Theme of Thomas Tallis* is explicitly reactionary, though with an originality of invention that Elgar, lacking Vaughan Williams's depth in musical scholarship and his familiarity with Tudor music, would have been pushed to match in that context. Vaughan Williams's *Sea Symphony*, coming in time exactly between the first and second symphonies of Elgar, is far rougher-hewn, less introverted and self-conscious, and reliant for its majesty upon sheer sound rather than structure. Though we instinctively regard Elgar as being definitively English, his is an England of pomp and circumstance, stateliness and comfort, whereas Vaughan Williams's conception of the place is derived from humbler materials. Elgar typifies Englishness in his reserve; much of the music of Vaughan Williams, at this period and later, has little or no reserve. Elgar, though, knew exactly how to create the effects he sought: Vaughan Williams was proceeding, if not by trial and error, then still somewhat experimentally. Both of them were pioneers, though in his rawness and his lack of reliance on the romantic tradition Vaughan Williams was more so than Elgar.

The first properly mature work by Vaughan Williams coincides with his return from Paris in 1908. He did not imitate Ravel: his teacher told him 'that I was the only pupil who "n'écrit pas de ma musique".' He knew he could not have written Ravel's music even if he had tried, for he was convinced he lacked the same power of invention. Also, devotion to English folk-song was too heavily upon him, Ravel lacking similar baggage. However, he was inspired not just about the manner of writing music, but the forms that writing should take. His first string quartet was written almost immediately upon his return to London in 'a bad attack of French fever'; and a new ease comes into Vaughan Williams's writing, a fluidity and confidence that suggest a breaking-out of creativity through some sort of self-imposed dam. None the less, a comparison with Ravel's own String Quartet in F of 1904 shows the Frenchman to have been light years ahead of his pupil in his command of harmonics and his daring use of rhythm.

Vaughan Williams then set to writing a song-cycle based on six of A. E. Housman's poems from *A Shropshire Lad*, whose title, taken from the first of the poems, was *On Wenlock Edge*. The cycle – originally for tenor, piano and string quartet, but later orchestrated in the composer's preferred setting – shows a new range to Vaughan Williams's musical thought, and is a further explicit testimony to the power of Ravel over him. In dealing with Housman's usual themes – premature death, loss and disappointment – the composer none the less injects passion, humour, beauty, pastorality as well as gloom into his music. Housman, an altogether more complicated fellow than the composer who set him and much more of a piece with his near contemporary and fellow Worcestershire man Elgar, hated it. To students of Vaughan Williams's music, however, the work reveals one of the greatest legacies of Ravel: that Vaughan Williams had learned how to paint with music, to suggest rich colour and texture through sound.

With his return to England, Vaughan Williams resumed his collecting of folk-songs. In late 1908 he was in Herefordshire, where he accumulated a particularly rich selection of carols. He had had a commission from Trinity College, too, to write music for the Greek play the following year, which was to be a performance of *The Wasps* of Aristophanes. This occupied him for much of the winter, along with continuing work on the symphony. The play, with the first performance of the incidental music, was staged in Cambridge in the autumn of 1909, shortly after the première of *On Wenlock Edge*. The work, especially the famous overture, reveals an almost Parry-like fluency and command of the musical vocabulary, the results again, ironically, of the inspiration and confidence given to the composer by Ravel; and it reveals that distinct voice, now fully rounded, that would trigger a host of imitations among some lesser English composers in the decades ahead. Before going to Ravel, Vaughan Williams had also written music for the performance of some scenes from Bunyan's *The Pilgrim's Progress*, a work whose mysticism was to become a leitmotif in the composer's creative life, and which he would make several attempts to set to music. From these early beginnings he sensed an opera could be made out of the story. In time it was, but it took him another forty years.

The great priority now, though, was the completion of *A Sea Symphony*. A performance had been scheduled for the Leeds Festival of October 1910, on the composer's thirty-eighth birthday, which meant the work's being finished early in the year; and he had the additional pressure of fulfilling a commission for the Three Choirs Festival the previous month, the first unequivocal sign that he had reached the front rank of the English musical scene. This commission for an orchestral work would bring forth the *Fantasia on a Theme of Thomas Tallis*. Writing with the ancient cathedral of Gloucester in mind, he built his fantasia round a psalm tune Tallis had written in 1567, and which in the *English Hymnal* became the hymn 'When rising from the bed of death'; the work is for a double string orchestra and a solo string quartet. The result is what many who have heard it consider to be the ultimate expression of the English soul in music; a wedding of the composer's understanding of polyphony and modal forms with his appreciation of the place of religion and religious institutions in English national life, creating an overall celestial effect. That it, and *A Sea Symphony*, appeared within weeks of each other in the autumn of 1910 suggested that Vaughan Williams had at last reached the highest level of creativity. The *Tallis Fantasia* also explicitly connected its composer with that most metaphysical of concepts, the spirit of England; and with it he had built a new landmark of English culture.

A Sea Symphony is a choral symphony in a way Beethoven's is not: there is singing throughout. It is hearty, robust, secular music, remarkably unpretentious, and must have been an intense shock to a public who associated English choral music with the reverential holiness of *Gerontius*, or the stateliness of *I Was Glad*. In its sound it is more like Parry than Elgar (despite the composer's protestations about what the symphony owed to *Gerontius*), but it is a radical departure from the styles of either man. The great fanfare with which the work begins, to be followed by the proclamation 'Behold, the sea itself!' from the choir, gave the composer, as he conducted the first performance, the feeling that he was about to be blown off the rostrum. The restlessness and might of the ocean are clearly depicted, so much so as to demand great energy not just from the orchestra and chorus, but from the listener too. Vaughan Williams was deeply nervous, and in a state of deep anxiety and agitation, before this debut of his first great work. He was dissatisfied with the performance, although the festival orchestra was comprised of first-rank professionals, many of whom had spent the summer season at Covent Garden. However, the work was acclaimed, and in time took its place in the repertoire. That the symphony worked as well as it did was greatly down to Hugh Allen, who taught music at Oxford and was a close friend of the composer's. Adrian Boult, who was introduced to Vaughan Williams by Allen and who as one of England's leading conductors would later become one of the greatest champions of his music, recalled the two men spending a whole day at Allen's house 'going through the string parts of *A Sea Symphony* and making them, well, playable. They were almost unplayable at Leeds and it was only that brilliant orchestra that could make a show of playing some of the extraordinarily intricate and difficult passages; and so the work was considerably simplified for its second performance.'

The impact it made did not just elevate to new heights the reputation of its composer; it announced the arrival of a new generation of musicians, following on from Parry and Elgar; for Holst was still at Vaughan Williams's side, and George Butterworth was leading an even younger group behind them. The freshness, vitality and exuberance of *A Sea Symphony* were symbolic, appropriately, of a new wave in English music. It steadily notched up performances; and after one in London in 1913 Vaughan Williams's friend Bruce Richmond, editor of the *Times Literary Supplement*, wrote to him to say simply that 'no one can say our generation hasn't accomplished anything first rate'. There was much joshing talk of the work's 'impertinences', its violation of what had hitherto been the polite norms of English – for which read German – choral music. This was not, however, because Vaughan Williams was out to shock; the effect was the result of his pent-up energy, his determination to represent in music the power and majesty of the ocean, but above all of the confidence newly instilled into him that his own voice, speaking in its own way, was as acceptable as any of the other more familiar tones to which the musical public had so long been used.

It was Butterworth, an Old Etonian former schoolmaster who had given up teaching to study at the RCM, to whom

Vaughan Williams credited the inspiration for his second symphony, the *London*. He had introduced Butterworth to the liberation theology of English folk-song, which he said had been Butterworth's 'salvation' from the shadows of Brahms and Schumann: it helped him 'to realise himself and to cast off the fetters of Teutonism'. Like Holst, Butterworth was a regular visitor to the Vaughan Williamses' house in Chelsea, and in about 1911 seems to have suggested to him that his next symphonic expression should be in the more usual orchestral form rather than choral. As the work progressed – and it did so slowly, as the *Sea* had – Vaughan Williams showed the sketches to Butterworth; and eventually dedicated the work to him. Its progress was slow because, as usual, the composer was engaged on other schemes: notably his first opera, *Hugh the Drover*, about life in a Cotswold village in the early nineteenth century.

Although he was becoming both prolific and successful, this rooting of his creativity very much not just in the soil of England but in its past differentiated him from Holst, who was pursuing far more innovative and unusual courses. This was not a problem; but it would for a time become one. He had, however backward-looking some of his work was, acquired the knack of writing beautiful and original music. Such, too, was the originality of a composer who had reverted to the modes for his means of composition that there was a great virtue in this atavism; but, with every novelty, there would come a time when it would be felt by others to have worn off. For the moment, though, there was still freshness in this means of musical expression, and in an England yet to lose so much of its innocence in the bloodbath of the Great War, still much undiluted pleasure to be had in looking back. There were as yet no painful contemporary realities for composers such as Vaughan Williams to have to observe and reflect in their music: that, however, would come all too soon.

The commission that followed on the success of the *Tallis Fantasia*, which was to write a piece for the Worcester Festival, resulted in the *Five Mystical Songs*, settings of divine poems by George Herbert for baritone solo, choir and orchestra. The music shows a new departure in being intensely sensuous, not least in the opening song *Easter*. It also gives another object lesson in the benefits of Ravel, with Vaughan Williams using the orchestra to create radical new sounds and exciting, unorthodox sensations, notably in the finale, *Antiphon*, the setting of the psalm 'Let all the world in every corner sing'. In some respects it is a work of greater genius even than the *Tallis Fantasia*, the composer brilliantly contrasting the forces of soloist, choir and orchestra. It would not always be held in high regard: after hearing a performance of it in 1934 the young Benjamin Britten, whose genius was unquestioned, wrote that 'the fifteen biblical songs of RVW finished me entirely; that "pi" and artificial mysticism combined with, what seems to me, technical incompetence sends me crazy'. His correspondent, Grace Williams, rebuked him sternly for this: 'Now don't malign poor old Uncle Ralph and call his mysticism artificial. There's nothing artificial about the man: I swear it; and I happen to know him pretty well. Those songs are absolutely sincere *and well scored.*'

Although such music as this settles the matter that

Vaughan Williams had his own distinct voice, the influence of folk-song upon him remained intense: indeed, it was what made it true to say that he had achieved his aim of becoming, by his definition of the term, an English composer. Lecturing in 1912, he told an audience that 'the evolution of the English folk song by itself has ceased but its spirit can continue to grow and flourish at the hands of our native composers'. It was the spirit that he was carrying on, and would carry on for years until such times as it became identical with his own style. In the new symphony which, according to his widow, he was writing 'with infinite struggle', the folk-song spirit would reveal itself in the cry of a lavender-seller used in the slow movement, and in the jollity of the opening movement. Yet, perhaps because the programme for the symphony is one of urban London, the presence of folk-song is not all that is visible. Ravel's fingerprints are on the scherzo, as are Stravinsky's and Debussy's, and the portrayals of the grandeur and bustle of the city have echoes of Elgar; the death march that opens the fourth movement is not entirely of this period; its starkness, and the starkness of its context, owes much to the drastic cutting of the symphony that Vaughan Williams undertook on his return from the Great War and after the death in battle of George Butterworth, its dedicatee.

His most notable work of 1912, the *Fantasia on Christmas Carols*, also owed much to folk-song, and was one of his most successful and original treatments of it. Using tunes gathered from Herefordshire and Sussex, the *Fantasia* evokes the wonder of the Christmas story and the traditional celebrations of it, while being laced with a strain of sadness that speaks of the full hardship of the winter in an age before

42

modern medicine, electric light and central heating. The piece exemplifies the serious treatment Vaughan Williams gave to folk-song material, and which he would probably only better in his *Five Variants of Dives and Lazarus* of 1939; simple songs placed in a sophisticated orchestral context that only highlighted and intensified their qualities rather than obscuring them. He was, though, making a reputation as a composer who drew greatly on traditional tunes and forms, and despite the broader range of his output as he became older, it was a reputation – or rather, in the light of later developments, a caricature – he would never entirely shake off.

Before the first performance of *A London Symphony* Vaughan Williams had another rare, but successful, journey into chamber music, this time with his *Phantasy Quintet*. It had its première on 23 March 1914; the symphony came four days later, at the Queen's Hall, and was a triumph. Holst, who was present, told his friend: 'You really have done it this time. Not only have you reached the heights, but you have taken your audience with you . . . I wish I could tell you how I and everyone else was carried away on Friday.' The symphony is glorious, big music, the grand tunes contained in every movement brimming with invention and confidence, the work at times overwhelming in its beauty and in its sensitivity as well as in its aesthetic force. Every bit as well as Elgar, Vaughan Williams conveys the spirit of England before the Great War – a real, tangible, everyday England glimpsed on the streets and in the squares of its capital city, not the mystical England of the *Tallis Fantasia*. The second, slow movement was 'Bloomsbury Square on a November afternoon'; the scherzo was meant to be an evening on the Westminster Embankment with the distant sounds of the Strand. The two movements framing these represented what Virginia Woolf later called 'the tramp and the trudge . . . the bellow and the uproar' of the city, though Vaughan Williams preferred the depiction, verging upon the mystical, of the city by H. G. Wells at the end of his novel *Tono-Bungay*, published in 1909: 'Light after light goes down. England and the Kingdom, Britain and the Empire, the old prides and the old devotions, glide abeam, astern, sink down upon the horizon, pass – pass. The river passes – London passes, England passes . . .'

George Butterworth, to whom the work owed so much, wrote of it afterwards that Vaughan Williams had at last given evidence of having overcome what another critic had called his 'impediment of musical speech'. 'It would be hard', Butterworth also wrote, 'to name any other first-rate composer who has "found himself" with such apparent difficulty as Vaughan Williams, and this fact is sometimes cited against him as a proof of amateurish clumsiness; the beauty and originality of his ideas is widely recognised, but the not infrequent failure to express them clearly is usually ascribed to some inherent incapacity for perfecting a technique.' In the *London*, Butterworth believed that, 'almost for the first time the composer's ideas and their actual expression are really commensurate'.

Despite the frequency with which his works were being performed, and despite his now undoubted eminence in English musical life, Vaughan Williams could not find an English publisher for the score of this impressive new work.

44

As a result, in the late spring of 1914 he sent the manuscript to a firm in Leipzig that had already published *Toward the Unknown Region* and *A Sea Symphony*. No copy was made: the composer could not face that expense, and he was too busy trying to complete his opera *Hugh the Drover* to do it himself. Fortunately for him, when it seemed a few weeks later that war might break out between Britain and Germany, Butterworth had the presence of mind to realise that the score might never be seen again. He therefore set about reconstructing a copy of the orchestral score from the individual parts that had been used at the first performance, enlisting other mutual friends as copyists.

As war became imminent *Hugh the Drover* was almost finished, and Vaughan Williams was working on a pastoral romance for orchestra inspired by George Meredith's poem 'The Lark Ascending'. The idylls of rural life and nature, like the carefree splendour and gaieties of London evoked in his new symphony, were however shortly to become an irrelevance. Work on his music would be suspended, to be resumed in a world unrecognisable by the standards of 1914, when a folk-opera seemed an understandable idea, and the activities of larks were still a legitimate object of artistic concern.

THREE

A Search for a Style

At the outbreak of war Vaughan Williams was nearly forty-two, an age at which those with no military training – like him – would normally expect to leave war to younger men. However, it was typical of his deep unselfishness that he was keen to serve. His first step was to join the special constabulary. However, within a few weeks he had managed to enlist in the Royal Army Medical Corps, which at least held out the prospect of his getting to the front. He was nearly disqualified because of flat feet, but so good were his other credentials that he was recruited to be a wagon orderly, where the state of his feet would not matter. He underwent some basic medical training in London and then did a period of stretcher drill in Dorking. He made an uncomfortable soldier, being much older than most of his comrades and from a very different background from others in the ranks; but he was popular, and happy, and it seems to have occurred neither to him nor to his superiors that he ought to be recommended for officer training. He embarked on his new duties with the sincerity and commitment he brought to his music, and which made it compelling.

A friend who saw him shortly before he joined up, sitting in the nave of Worcester Cathedral with his wife, memorably described the image of the composer at this time: the sun shone through the windows on Adeline's hair 'which looked like pure gold . . . He had a thick thatch of dark hair, a tall, rather heavy figure, even then slightly bowed; and his face was profoundly moving, deep humanity and yet with the quality of a mediaeval sculpture.'

Once in the army, his musical activities were limited to playing the organ for church parades, or accompanying other soldiers for sing-songs. The army was not quick to exploit the sacrifice this eminent man was making for his country. He spent all of 1915 in England, in Hertfordshire and north Essex, and at the start of 1916 moved to Wiltshire. It was not until 22 June, nine days before the opening of the Battle of the Somme and the blackest day in the history of the British army, that the Field Ambulance finally left for Le Havre. In a letter to Holst, who (having been ruled medically unfit for military service) was still pursuing his career as music master at St Paul's Girls School in London, he wrote on arrival that 'I am very well and enjoy my work . . . I am "waggon orderly" and go up the line every night to bring back wounded and sick in a motor ambulance.' He wrote no music, but ideas began to germinate in his mind, notably one which would after the war become his third symphony, the *Pastoral*. He described that work, in spite of its title, as being 'really war-time music . . . it's not really lambkins frisking at all as most people take for granted'. While the unit had been in Essex, at Saffron Walden, Vaughan Williams had formed a choir, and once the unit was in France the choir continued under his direction, welcoming anyone who wished to join.

He was happier to be getting on with the war, doing something practical rather than simply drilling, despite the horror of what he witnessed in Flanders. Butterworth's death, and that of his brother-in-law Charles Fisher at the Battle of Jutland, brought home to him in the summer of 1916 just what a different world he would return to; and since he had a preponderance of friends from Butterworth's generation, the gaps in his life would be stark. As well as being devastated by her brother's death, Adeline Vaughan Williams, though only in her late forties, was already stricken with the arthritis that would render her an invalid for much of the rest of her life. Even for one whose character was as strong, optimistic and selfless as Vaughan Williams's, life was taking on more sombre tones. In this context, however, his belief in the missionary activities of music and musicians became all the stronger, as a means of preserving civilisation in the midst of an era of carnage and social upheaval. He told Holst in June 1916, with relation to his work at St Paul's Girls School and Morley College for working men, that 'I sometimes feel that the future of musical England rests with you – because every Paulina who goes out, & for the matter of that every Morleyite, will infect 10 others & they in their turn will infect 10 others – I will leave you to make the necessary calculation.' It was precisely the belief that was to drive him on after the war, not just to resume composing, but to teach and to encourage others to make music; it would provide him with the reason eventually to lead England's musical life.

In the autumn of 1916 his unit was entrained south for

Marseilles, where they were put on a boat for Salonika, to provide medical assistance in the fight against Turkey. The change of scene was for a time entertaining, and the choir was trained up to sing the carols Vaughan Williams had collected in Herefordshire and Sussex, only this time in the valley beneath Mount Olympus. However, by early in 1917 he was bored and frustrated with what his friend and fellow composer Arthur Bliss called 'the drudgery of a private's work with the RAMC'. His main duty in Greece was to fill in puddles of water to stop mosquitoes breeding in them, which hardly constituted the best use of his education and abilities. At last, it was arranged for him to return to England and undergo officer training. While at home that summer he was gratified to note the regular performances of his works, including both symphonies, in London and elsewhere. Meanwhile, he dutifully went through cadet school, and passed out with his commission in November 1917. It was not until the following March that he left for France again, now a subaltern (aged forty-five) in the Royal Artillery, and (after extensive gunnery training) in charge of 200 horses.

At the end of the war, from which he emerged physically unscathed, Vaughan Williams wrote to Holst that, far from sharing in the jubilation of the Armistice, he had suffered 'a complete slump in my mind, and I've never felt so fed up with my job'. He had to start the arduous process of moving his horses back to England; but at the end of 1918 he was rescued from that task by his appointment as director of music for the First Army. With the fighting over but total demobilisation some way off, the army realised it had to provide recreational and creative opportunities for its men;

and music was one of them. Vaughan Williams set up new choirs, bands and an orchestra, and had managed to establish something passing for a musical life among his comrades by the time he was himself demobilised in February 1919. Reviving his own, at a much higher level, would not be so easy.

Holst had, just before the end of the war, managed to find his own role as part of a war effort from which he had throughout been excluded. He took up a post organising music abroad for the YMCA, and he too had gone to Salonika. In his absence Adrian Boult had given the first public performance of *The Planets*, whose astonishing originality and beauty confirmed the genius of a man who had long felt himself to be in Vaughan Williams's shadow, and initiated the most fruitful period in Holst's life. The great popular success this work would bring Holst, and the international acclaim that would accompany him until the end of his life, were his due, and never remotely resented by his close friend and fellow composer. However, for the next few years Vaughan Williams would find himself from time to time a little overshadowed by Holst, and certainly not always his match in creativity.

The reason for this stuttering in Vaughan Williams's progress – which may best be seen as a momentary loss of direction, or a failure for a while to orientate himself satisfactorily in the much changed postwar world – while Holst flowered may lie in their different wartime experiences. Mr Kennedy has observed that 'I believe that the First World War had more effect on him than he would admit', and an examination of the nature of his works in the next decade especially reinforces the truth of that observation. He rarely talked of the war, his music serving as the outlet for the feelings provoked by it. Before 1914 Vaughan Williams showed signs of pursuing ideas and influences other than those prompted by folk-song, broadening the range of his musical thought. *Hugh the Drover* was indisputably backward-looking; but although the subject-matter of the other work in progress, *The Lark Ascending*, was unequivocally pastoral, there is nothing predictable or stereotypical about the writing for the violin that describes the lark's progress.

What Vaughan Williams had seen in Flanders had left its mark on him, and in more ways than just the variation of the *Last Post* we hear in the *Pastoral Symphony*, a work that may justly be regarded as his 'war requiem'. In the years immediately after the war, there was too much looking back, and apparently not enough of an attempt to try to confront what was happening in the new, changed world to which Vaughan Williams had come back but which Holst had never really left. With his long-standing interest in the Orient and mysticism, Holst was in any case subject to wider and more challenging influences than his friend, and this had shown in *The Planets*. English musical life was, however, now largely up to these two men. With Parry, to Vaughan Williams's great sorrow, dying just before the Armistice, Elgar about to be virtually silenced by his grief at the death of his wife, and the likes of Moeran, Bliss and Warlock struggling for recognition further down the line, the lead was now theirs to take. When Elgar's first works after the war – notably the Cello Concerto – were met with a critical hostility that seemed to stem from a reaction against Edwardian conceptions of nobility, beauty and style, the field was clearly open for the next generation.

Adrian Boult identified the nature of the change the war wrought on music. 'We now want our music shorter and more terse; we seem to need a sharper difference in style between the dramatic and the symphonic; and our composers usually write for smaller orchestras and on a smaller scale.' He said this with reference to Elgar, who would write barely anything in the last fifteen years of his life, saying 'goodbye to the Edwardian style of opulence and magnificence'. Although Vaughan Williams had not been as guilty of such indulgence as Elgar, such tones had been audible in both symphonies, and had lent them a great self-confidence and presence. Now, instead, there was to be a period if not of self-doubt, then certainly of readjustment and reflection. What had seemed to composers such as Vaughan Williams to be the certainties of life before the war now barely existed.

The Vaughan Williamses spent the spring and summer of 1919 in a cottage on the Norfolk coast. He embarked on his revision of *A London Symphony*, shortening it, darkening it, and dedicating it posthumously to Butterworth. Boult called his excisions from the symphony 'ruthless', cutting out as the composer did some seven or eight minutes. Vaughan Williams tinkered with *Hugh the Drover*; and he began to write his third symphony, which was to be the main receptacle for the outpourings of his experiences in the war. Parry's successor as director of the RCM, Hugh Allen, invited Vaughan Williams to teach there from the autumn of 1919, as part-time professor of composition. There had been a move to have Vaughan Williams succeed Parry, but he made it clear that he wished, now, to concentrate on composition rather than administration and running the College: an exhausting task that Parry had accepted out of a sense of duty, and which it was felt had badly harmed not just his career as a composer, but also his health. That Vaughan Williams's reputation had grown in his absence on active service was clear when, that summer, Oxford made him a Doctor of Music *honoris causa*. The Public Orator spoke of 'his great services to English music' and added that 'he had developed a style of his own which placed him in the front rank of English composers'. Yet it was also indubitably the case that, with Elgar moving out of favour and Parry dead, that front rank was looking pretty depleted.

Vaughan Williams's assumption of a place at the head of English music was mainly down to his peculiar talent and his original application of it: but the appointment of Allen to the RCM, which enabled the appointment in turn of Vaughan Williams to teach there, was also crucial. A generation of students was brought up in the mould of the English school that Vaughan Williams, Holst and Allen now so actively represented. It was not just the new influences from the continent, from Stravinsky onwards, that this school would push to one side: it would also be responsible for part of the at times brutal reassessment made of Elgar, though not through any deliberate move of Vaughan Williams's, who had a healthy respect for the older man. Also, some musicians from a younger generation who did not conform either musically or politically, such as the brilliant John Foulds, would find it increasingly hard to have a hearing. Not until much later in the twenties and in the early thirties, when the continental influences proved too strong to resist, would it be possible for men such as Walton and Britten – helped again by a large share of genius – to counter the new English orthodoxy. Nor was it just his musical abilities that gave Vaughan Williams such power over a whole musical generation: the great sincerity and selflessness with which he conducted his campaign of artistic evangelism gave him a huge moral authority that simply cemented his place as the musical establishment's leader.

Sharing his recognition and good fortune with a friend who had supported him even in the darkest days, Holst dedicated his *Hymn of Jesus* to Vaughan Williams; it was first performed in March 1920, and was another great popular success. Vaughan Williams, for his part, continued to try to work out influences from the past. He started work on a theme from Bunyan, which had been with him mentally for the last fifteen years, and which would emerge as the one-act 'pastoral episode' *The Shepherds of the Delectable Mountains*. Nor could he break away from ideas of polyphony: for the choir of Westminster Cathedral he wrote his *Mass in G Minor*. 'There is no reason', he put it sensibly, 'why an atheist could not write a good Mass.' Inevitably there is a sobriety and contemplativeness in the Mass, and those qualities may be down to more than just the demands of such a piece of music. In its tone the Mass presages what is probably Vaughan Williams's finest work of the decade, the oratorio *Sancta Civitas*, though by the time the composer came to write that he was becoming increasingly less constrained by the musical conventions of the past. In June 1920 Marie Hall, the dedicatee, was the soloist in the first performance of *The*

Lark Ascending. For all its beauty, redolent of an England that no longer existed, it presented a sharp contrast with the bold, almost pioneering move forward musically that Holst was taking. There is a pervasive, and appropriate, darkness about much of Holst's writing at this time that conveys a perceptible chill: the *Lark* is still full of sunlight and warmth, which sit less easily with the times.

As well as teaching and composing, Vaughan Williams threw himself more energetically into conducting: not just his own works, but also as musical director of the Bach Choir, a post he assumed early in 1921. A lover of Bach's music almost above any other, he had sung in the choir for fifteen years, and took on these responsibilities with genuine enthusiasm. He immediately set about not just developing the choir, but also expanding its repertoire; and he was able to promote some of Holst's work too. To judge from the accounts of those who played in orchestras under him, Vaughan Williams's skill as a conductor did not match his enthusiasm, and many professional players found that they often had to decide for themselves where and at what speed they should be going. Since, however, Vaughan Williams himself appears to have had no illusions or pretensions about his abilities, he never forfeited the affections of the orchestras he conducted, despite his occasional, and famous, rages that would be unleashed in moments of frustration; and would just as quickly subside again.

On 26 January 1922 the first fruits of the composer's wartime experiences, *A Pastoral Symphony*, had its first performance in a concert conducted by Boult at the Queen's Hall. By now Vaughan Williams (who was, after all, in his fiftieth year) was a sufficiently significant figure for the arrival of a new symphony to be a great event: and its two predecessors were by now becoming quite well known and were a big part of the basis of his reputation. The work was an instant success; but it was of a very different colour from the *Sea* and the *London*. It was deeply reflective, and its pastorality owed nothing to folk-song. The composer's assertion that this was music of the war, of the tortured landscape of northern France, is felt at once by the listener to be true. He told Boult when he was writing the symphony that 'I've got a new tune and it's in four movements and they are all slow. I don't think anybody will like it much.' So lacking in confidence about it was Vaughan Williams that he urged Boult, during the rehearsals, to see it was played much faster than the conductor had imagined it ought to be. For the first few years this would characterise his interpretation of it. Then, Vaughan Williams heard a performance under Boult and said to him: 'You know, you're doing it terribly fast. Every movement's really faster than I want.' When Boult reminded him of his earlier injunction, the composer replied: 'I've conducted it a bit and I've heard it a good deal now since those days. I realise that it isn't so boring to people as I thought it was going to be.'

The joke of Peter Warlock's that the music was that of a cow looking over a gate, or even Hugh Allen's observation that it represented 'VW rolling over and over in a ploughed field on a wet day' suggest that both men missed the point about the genesis of the music. There could, after all, be no clearer clue than the mis-sounding of the octave of the *Last Post* in the second movement, echoing a mistake made by a bugler in Vaughan Williams's hearing while on Salisbury Plain. Yet the composer invited misinterpretation by giving such a name to the symphony. The expression in the first movement is not so much of physical beauty as of calm, though it is a calm made overwhelming, almost oppressive, by some thick orchestral textures. It is then dispelled by the darker tone of the second movement, such calm as survives being that of mourning rather than contentment. At the moment when the *Last Post* is deliberately misquoted, the image is unquestionably one of lines of white headstones.

Then the third movement brings a surprise. A scherzo, it has the subdued tone of the rest of the symphony, never escaping into sheer joy; but it is a sophisticated, grand tune redolent of a Spanish dance that lifts the whole work, before a finale that, with its plaintive soprano intervention, restores not merely a mood of contemplation, but one of mysticism and other-worldliness. With three slow movements and a fourth that barely gets out of third gear, the symphony can hardly be arresting in any conventional way; its beauty, dignity and sincerity are not, however, in question, and are captivating in themselves. It is best seen as one man's attempt – broadly successful – to come to terms with the worst war in modern history, and with the wiping out of a generation that included both family and friends. What it says about the world that is left is more dark than light, the exuberance of the pre-war works having been all but snuffed out, to be recalled in a nostalgic melancholy discernible in the symphony's scherzo. In that respect, it was a more contemporary work than its critics at the time, and many who have listened to it since, would concede. As with other works that would shortly follow it – notably *Sancta Civitas* – there is a sense of the composer being weighed down by his recent experiences, rather than jumping up to challenge them and conquer them as he would be felt to do in the thirties and forties.

Four

Mature Mysticism

As can be gathered from his comments on the Mass, Vaughan Williams had not had any sort of religious experience as a result of his war. He and his wife went to North America for the first time in the early summer of 1922, partly to give the first American performance of *A Pastoral Symphony*, and he wrote to Holst to say that 'I have seen (a) Niagara and (b) the Woolworth buildings, and am most impressed by (b). I've come to the conclusion that the works of Man terrify me more than the Works of God.' Once home again his life was occupied more in teaching and administration than, for the moment, in writing; though he wrote a short score for a ballet, *Old King Cole*, commissioned by the Cambridge branch of the English Folk Dance Society, which was first performed in June 1923. The following month the Royal Military School of Music gave the first performance of what has become one of his best-known pieces, the *English Folk Song Suite*, in its original conception for military band. As with so many of the composer's treatments of folk-song, the application of his particular musical genius to them transforms these old peasant tunes into a passionate exposition of the English soul: not least in the cheerful Somerset tune collected by Cecil Sharp that begins the suite, *Seventeen Come Sunday*.

His next major work, however, was not at all in this vein, and would come to represent a turning-point in his creative development: the oratorio *Sancta Civitas*. He worked at it in the summer of 1923, at the same time as he was orchestrating *On Wenlock Edge*, putting that song-cycle into the form he would always prefer. Performances of his earlier works were now occurring with greater and greater frequency, thanks largely to the championship of Boult, and within a year of its first performance *A Pastoral Symphony* was taken up as a popular work. Its success, however, did little to reassure its composer about the departure he would shortly take into a different musical sphere.

Having now worked at *Hugh the Drover* for the best part of fifteen years, Vaughan Williams was having problems bringing to parturition a work that, for all its charm and undeniably beautiful music, had the appearance of being almost as out of place in the harsh postwar world as the grand Edwardian tunes of Elgar. However, in the early summer of 1924 it was at last being rehearsed by both the RCM and the British National Opera Company. The composer was beset with anxiety about its first performance, which was scheduled at the RCM on 4 July. This, and the three other performances given there in the next week, seems to have been successful, despite the reservations and fears the composer and some of his circle appear to have had in advance; but when the BNOC came to perform the opera, at His Majesty's Theatre under the young but fast-rising conductor Malcolm Sargent, it suffered from a lack of rehearsal.

Although revived several times in the succeeding quarter-century, it has never had a secure place in the repertoire in England, let alone outside it. Sargent was, however, to have a long and fruitful partnership with Vaughan Williams, especially as a missionary on his behalf, taking his symphonies around the world. He also recorded extracts from *Hugh* shortly after its first performances, an important step for both composer and conductor.

The problems with *Hugh* are not just that it was folksy at a time when there was little public mood for such things, being an excursion into the Merrie England of the Napoleonic era, complete with its ballad-seller, turnkey, cheap-jack and primrose-seller. The British taste for opera, then as now, was for the standards and style set by the European masters. For all the excellence of its music, *Hugh* cannot but appear provincial or parochial, stripped of the mystery and exotic romance that audiences had come to expect after a diet of Verdi and Puccini. Its libretto, by Harold Child, a journalist, is perhaps most kindly described as naive. Never much more than one-dimensional, it robs the opera of such emotional depth as the composer might have wanted it to have, and does the drama no favours at all. Sadly for Vaughan Williams, he was to learn fewer lessons than he should have from the difficulties with this work, and the problems of its acceptance by the public; and his failure to do so would provide a recurring theme of disappointment throughout a career of growing acclaim whenever he tried to take on and beat the received wisdom in his own country about opera.

By the mid-twenties it could legitimately be felt that while Vaughan Williams's technique had matured, and while his capacity to invent tunes and capture moods of reflectiveness was that of a first-rate composer, his range was seeming somewhat limited, his invention closeted not merely in the English countryside, but in an England before the war. In every respect he was established: the Oxford University Press now published his music, so there was no need to comb Europe looking for a publisher. With the greater availability of his scores, so performances of his works multiplied, often with the composer as conductor. He started to make a decent income from his music, some of which he used to finance new undertakings such as a performance of *The Shepherds of the Delectable Mountains*.

His style was not entirely entrenched, however, and already there are signs of his breaking out of the boundaries he seems to have set around himself. Some of the songs he wrote in the twenties show a more modern inspiration, stripped of some of the obvious and predictable cosiness of the world of folk-song. Not least, in this respect, were the 1925 settings of poems by Adeline's niece Fredegond Shove, a wholly unexceptional poet but whose words in songs such as *Four Nights* are given passion and flavour by Vaughan Williams's music. These settings owe nothing to folk-song, as some of his earlier ones had, but have more of the intimacy and worldliness of German *lieder* about them, with great evidence of originality and musical development. The piano accompaniment is more consciously chromatic, challenging the voice rather than providing simply an obligatory backdrop for it.

The range of Vaughan Williams's musical interests was not a limiting factor upon him. On a visit to Prague in 1925 he heard and enjoyed Janáček's *The Cunning Little Vixen*; but, in the same year, he could not grasp Holst's new *Choral Symphony*, something quite different in its conception of choral music from any of the more traditional exercises in the form that Vaughan Williams had made, and shot through with a darkness that his friend, even in his own moments of reflection, would not have been able to understand. Giving Holst the benefit of the doubt, Vaughan Williams suspected the choir had not understood the work, and that its execution had suffered accordingly. He wrote to Holst after the first performance to say that 'I shall live in faith till I have heard it again several times and then I shall find out what a bloody fool I was not to see it all the first time.' It is not an easy work; but it is one that exemplifies Holst's innovative and radical style, one that someone of Vaughan Williams's personal musical conservatism (he was, ironically, not a conservative in any other way) was clearly struggling to appreciate. The general critical view was, however, with Vaughan Williams; it was fifty years before the work was first recorded, by Boult, then in his mid-eighties.

Characteristically, Vaughan Williams pursued his own attempts at innovation in a more cautious and less confrontational way than Holst. Inspired by the *Song of Solomon*, he composed a suite for his favourite instrument, the viola, entitled *Flos Campi*. In the context of his own work, it was a radical departure, a sign of greater flexibility to come, and of a willingness to experiment. Though at times unsubtle and a little thickly orchestrated, it depicts its biblical theme perfectly, with moments of intense sensuality. It is also at times self-consciously arty, particularly in the wordless chorus, which will inevitably strike many listeners as unsatisfactory.

63

In dealing with an implicitly sexual text, the composer seems at times to have been conscious not of his own embarrassment, but perhaps of that of a few of his listeners, with the result that some of the musical effects can seem mildly arch.

Holst, whose experimentalism was less self-conscious, felt much the same about *Flos Campi* as Vaughan Williams had felt about his choral symphony. 'I couldn't get hold of Flos a bit and was therefore disappointed with it and me,' Holst wrote to him after the first performance in October 1925. It is a work that divides Vaughan Williams's admirers like few others; it is the perfect example, however, of the struggles he was still having to reorientate himself in middle age, between conflicting influences of the English past and the international present and future – not least, again, Ravel. It seems the composer was striving to make an individual statement in a different idiom, while constrained within a straitjacket of his own well-defined style and suffering a temporary lapse of self-confidence. It is, though, the first manifestation of the stylistic leap forward that would come within a few years.

Another sign of this desire to move on came within a month, with the first performance, by the Hungarian violinist Jelly d'Arányi, of Vaughan Williams's short Violin Concerto. The original title of the work, *Concerto Accademico*, might suggest that this is another retrospective exercise, with overtones of the eighteenth century. In some respects it is a homage to Bach, with the rigid disciplines and structures of his writing being sometimes evident. However, elsewhere the violin has work to do that takes it far from that earlier age; it is an example of how Vaughan Williams (like Stravinsky in a similar neo-classical context) would use the form of the concerto to stretch the instrument, to experiment with it and, if necessary, to be abrasive. As with the astonishing *Piano Concerto* of seven years later, there is a refreshing lack of predictability about what the solo instrument is expected to do, with a sense of impatience attacking the listener from the opening bars. Above all, there is a paradoxical lack of conformity to type for a piece that originally had the most conformist and typical conception. This is not entirely surprising; the second movement had originally been written as part of a Concerto Grosso for military band, which the composer scrapped, and the main theme in the finale is cribbed from *Hugh the Drover*. It is not, though, a nakedly emotional statement in the way that other great English violin concertos are – those of Elgar, Walton, Britten and Moeran, for example – and in that respect it is a missed opportunity, a work conveying a sense of sterility.

At this time, too, Vaughan Williams exerted a new, traditionalist grip on English musical life. Having infused his musical creed and ideas into the soul of the nation twenty years earlier with the *English Hymnal*, in 1925 he edited a new hymn book, *Songs of Praise*, for ecumenical purposes. This was widely used in schools and by the new British Broadcasting Company in its daily religious services, so bringing the mainstream of English music – as Vaughan Williams and his colleagues had defined it – home to an immensely wide audience. Then, in 1928, he edited the *Oxford Book of Carols*, with similar effect. Both works used, as the *English Hymnal* had done, traditional and polyphonic tunes, and drove out forcibly the early and mid-Victorian hymn tunes that Vaughan Williams regarded as sentimental, ghastly and unduly Germanic in tone. Although there was a logic in bringing English music into English worship, it can just as easily – though not so fairly – be argued that Vaughan Williams had merely substituted one form of sentimentality for another.

In the spring of 1926, during the General Strike, this atheist's latest religious – or, more accurately, religiose – work, the oratorio *Sancta Civitas,* was given its first performance. His widow said it was the choral of work of his that he liked the best, and it can claim to be the finest work of any description the composer had done since the war. Like *A Pastoral Symphony* before it, this vision of the Holy City is underpinned by the sadness and the suffering of a whole generation that had lost its innocence. A quotation from Plato – Socrates' meditation on the survival of the soul from *Phaedo* – with which the score is superscribed reads in part: 'That these things, or something like them, are true concerning the souls of men and their habitations after death, especially since the soul is shown to be immortal, this seems to me fitting and worth risking to believe. For the risk is honourable and a man should sing such things in the manner of an incantation to himself.' It is mysticism again, but mature mysticism: a struggle by a non-believer after such a terrible war to find some cause to believe that the soul might, after all, live on.

The oratorio's words are from Revelations and from Taverner's Bible. Much of the special atmosphere of the piece is established by a boys' choir, placed at a distance and giving it a heavenly aspect, and a distant trumpet used to similar purposes. It is, for the form, a remarkably short work, only just over half-an-hour long. Elgar was an early admirer, confiding in Vaughan Williams that he had thought of setting the words himself, but felt his younger colleague had done the job adequately for him. Although *Sancta Civitas* lacks the scope of *The Kingdom* and *The Apostles*, it packs much intensity and feeling into its short duration, and is scored for large orchestral and choral forces; and above all, in an uncharacteristic (for this era) use of dissonance, it conveys a brooding, almost radical sentiment of darkness and uncertainty from its opening bar. The austerity for which early critics attacked it can now be seen as one of its great qualities; and a quality that neither limits its beauty nor divorces it from realism. It is a work that has attained popularity among the composer's admirers only in recent years, helped by at least one magnificent recording; but its relevance now shows how ahead of its time the oratorio was, and, in retrospect, what a crucial break it represents for the composer with influences that can be seen, elsewhere in his music, to have held him back and created a sense of sterility. Some important later works – the short opera *Riders to the Sea* and the cantata *Dona Nobis Pacem* chief among them – can be heard to have their roots in *Sancta Civitas*, and a new chapter is opened by it in Vaughan Williams's creativity – even though part of *Sancta Civitas* had its roots in a discarded work of 1908. He is, for the first time, not afraid to be disturbing.

What discernible hints the oratorio gave at the time about this change of direction were not quickly followed up. Apart from a few songs and a *Te Deum*, it would be nearly three years before a new work of comparable significance came from Vaughan Williams: then, ironically, it would be the opera on which he spent much of the years 1924 to 1928 immersed in writing, *Sir John in Love*. Although in many ways *Sir John* is more convincing than *Hugh*, it none the less looked back in its hearty romanticism to the old values and techniques it had seemed the composer was putting behind him in *Sancta Civitas*. He had since 1925 been working on his one-act opera based on J.M. Synge's *Riders to the Sea*, an altogether more inventive work, had completed the *Te Deum*, had begun his Piano Concerto and was now embarked upon his *Benedicite*. Since before the war he had been contemplating *Sir John in Love*, based on the story of Falstaff.

The text was taken from *The Merry Wives of Windsor*, and for pillaging Shakespeare the composer said in his programme note that 'my only excuse is that he is fair game, like the Bible, and may be made use of nowadays even for advertisements of soap and razors'. He acknowledged a direct debt to Holst, who had used the same story in his opera *At the Boar's Head*. In Vaughan Williams's hands, the tale became one told with the help of folk-tunes, though these, as he himself admitted, accounted for not much more than fifteen minutes' music out of two hours. None the less, their use, even sparingly, gave the music a sense of predictability in the ears of those critics who (despite the compelling evidence of *Sancta Civitas*) felt that Vaughan Williams had come to be about the rarefied use of folk-song and little else. It was as if the composer's willingness to engage with the world around him, demonstrated in that oratorio, had been but an experiment, and that now there was to be, instead, a retreat into the comfortable and the familiar.

Almost the only discernible grievance Vaughan Williams

had about his music was that his operas were not taken more seriously, or given more professional performances. In her biography of him his widow suggests that this neglect might have stemmed from the early performances of his operas often being given by student companies, such as at the RCM, thereby creating the impression that they were geared to amateurs. In the case of *Hugh the Drover* and *Sir John in Love* there may be other reasons concerned with their suitability as operas; *Riders to the Sea*, which was not shackled by the English folk-song tradition, would emerge as an altogether different project, and one far less deserving of the critical cold-shoulder. Fundamentally, it would not be until the coming of Britten, harnessed as his genius was to currents in the European mainstream, that English opera ceased in the eyes and ears of the musical public to be a contradiction in terms.

It is perhaps at this juncture in his career, when the last work to judge him by was *Sir John in Love*, that the gap opening up between Vaughan Williams and some of his brothers-in-arms might have appeared most glaring. The critics and the public were not to know that three of the works in progress, the passionate and percussive Piano Concerto, the highly innovative *Riders to the Sea* and the majestic orchestral masque *Job*, would all show that it was *Sir John*, and not *Sancta Civitas*, that was the stylistic aberration. Holst, by comparison, was in a new phase of exploration, the high point of which would be his arresting and intense *Hammersmith – a Prelude and Scherzo for Orchestra*. Walton, in 1928 still only twenty-six, was embarking on his viola concerto (which Lionel Tertis, for whom Vaughan Williams had written *Flos Campi*, would reject because of its 'modernity') as a prelude to *Belshazzar's Feast*. In the obscurity of Paris, where he was earning a living accompanying silent films, John Foulds was working on his *Dynamic Triptych*, a tightly disciplined but pyrotechnic experiment in colour and rhythm, punctuated by silences and quarter-tones, which has a strong claim to be the greatest piano concerto yet written by a British composer. English music was moving on, the parochialism Vaughan Williams (and, for that matter, Holst) had been accused of imposing on it ever more a matter of fantasy, and Vaughan Williams himself, whatever may have seemed to be the case at the time, would not be left washed up on the beach when the tide went out.

The composer himself was conscious that some of the priorities of his life might need to be reordered, for personal as well as artistic reasons. In February 1928 he resigned his musical directorship of the Bach Choir. Though he had enjoyed his work, not least its evangelical aspects, and had been able to promote the music of English composers less fortunate than himself, he was being left with less and less time to write music. Also, his wife was increasingly living the life of an invalid, her health having taken a bad turn in 1927 when she broke a thigh so badly that she had to be encased in plaster from her chest downwards. The couple decided they must leave London and the home they had had for nearly twenty-five years at 13 Cheyne Walk, Chelsea. They began looking for a suitable house somewhere around Dorking in the Surrey hills, the area Vaughan Williams knew so well from his childhood.

He did not plan to abandon London altogether; he would continue to teach at the RCM, not least because he enjoyed the company of the younger generation. However, in the summer of 1929 the Vaughan Williamses finally moved out of London, taking a long lease on a bungalow on the outskirts of Dorking that they rechristened The White Gates. This became the base of the composer's activity during what would be the prime of his creative life; and it was ironic that, just as he based himself in the countryside, his work should immediately take on a distinctly less bucolic aspect.

FIVE

'Ultimately National'

When critics have looked for the earliest signs of the passion, anger and violence that, as if from nowhere, emerge from the Fourth and Sixth symphonies, they have usually traced them back to *Job: A Masque for Dancing*. Vaughan Williams's cousin Gwen Raverat was designing scenery and costumes for a dance envisaged by Geoffrey Keynes based on William Blake's illustrations for the Book of Job; and in 1927 Keynes had invited Vaughan Williams to write the music. For one so often inspired by the Bible this was an appealing task to be set, and his only condition was that the music would be 'a masque for dancing' and not a ballet, since he disliked that form of dance. The work was completed as an orchestral suite because of problems with the choreographic produc- tion, and first performed in Norwich in October 1930, conducted by the composer.

Since he had been aware that he would not in the first instance be writing for an orchestra that had to go in a theatre pit, he wrote the suite for a large orchestra, enabling him to create a majesty of sound and a gravity of tone still unusual in his work, though apparent to an extent in *Sancta*

BORDERS
BOOKS AND MUSIC
ROSEMONT SHOPPING CENTER
1149 LANCASTER AVE
BRYN MAWR PA 19010

STORE: 0030   REG: 04/21   TRAN#: 8339
SALE   09/06/2001   EMP: 00113

VAUGHAN WILLIAMS
     6478110   CL T   26.95
CKOX CONDUCTS VAUGHAN WILLIA
     6332894   CD T   16.99

           Subtotal   43.94
           PA 6% TAX   2.64
  Items   Total   46.58
           MASTERCARD   46.58
CT # /S XXXXXXXXXXXXX1374
               AUTH: 045463
ME: MORGAN MD/VERNON W

CUSTOMER COPY

09/06/2001 01:45PM

THANK YOU FOR SHOPPING AT BORDERS
PLEASE ASK ABOUT OUR SPECIAL EVENTS
        (610) 527-1500

sit our website at www.borders.com!

- Periodicals and newspapers may not be returned.
- Items purchased by check may be returned for cash after 10 business days.
- All returned checks will incur a $15 service charge.
- All other refunds will be granted in the form of the original payment.

BORDERS

- Returns must be accompanied by the original receipt
- Returns must be completed within 30 days.
- Merchandise must be in salable condition.
- Opened videos, discs and cassettes may be exchanged for replacement copies of the original items only.
- Periodicals and newspapers may not be returned.
- Items purchased by check may be returned for cash after 10 business days.
- All returned checks will incur a $15 service charge.
- All other refunds will be granted in the form of the original payment.

BORDERS

- Returns must be accompanied by the original receipt
- Returns must be completed within 30 days.
- Merchandise must be in salable condition.
- Opened videos, discs and cassettes may be exchanged for replacement copies of the original items only.
- Periodicals and newspapers may not be returned.
- Items purchased by check may be returned for cash after 10 business days.
- All returned checks will incur a $15 service charge.
- All other refunds will be granted in the form of the original payment.

Civitas. In using such large forces he risked stumbling because of his old Achilles heel, orchestration. Holst was at the Norwich rehearsal, and Arthur Bliss, sitting next to him, recalled his listening with 'frightening intensity'. At one point Holst announced, 'That doesn't come off. I must tell him,' and went up to speak to Vaughan Williams on the platform. The composer spoke to the players, and amendments were made. 'The section', Bliss recalled, 'was then tried over again, but with what a difference of sound! – clarity instead of thick obscurity. Holst always probed like a fine surgeon to the root of the difficulty.' For all Holst's influence, there is still what contemporary critics (taking their cue from the composer himself in his pre-Ravel days) called the 'lumpiness' of Vaughan Williams's rhythm, a contrast to the lightness of touch that Holst seemed to have developed from instinct. However, it is not so clear as in some works from the previous decade – it provides to some ears an almost fatal flaw in *Flos Campi*, depending on the taste of the listener – and would decline further in the years ahead.

At once a greater command of orchestration is apparent in the music of *Job*, as well as a profound emotional intensity not always obvious in Vaughan Williams's work before, and not really heard since his oratorio. The composer was quite open about the fact that he had 'cribbed' Satan's Dance 'deliberately from the scherzo of Beethoven's last quartet' – just as he would soon say he had taken the opening of his F Minor Symphony from the finale of the same composer's Ninth Symphony. 'I have never had any conscience about cribbing.' In its composition as in the final adjustments during rehearsals, Holst was especially important. 'I should be alarmed to say how many "field days" we spent over it,' Vaughan Williams recalled. There is much in the tone of the work that declares a debt to Holst, not least at times to *Hammersmith*, his most recently completed work and one of his most brilliant and enduring compositions. There is no doubt that Vaughan Williams overstressed the shortcomings in his technique, faults more than outweighed by the power of his invention; and that he could at times, as a result, be his own worst public relations man. Equally, the crystal clarity of Holst and the economy of Holst's scoring were facets of his friend's music from which he could, and did, learn much.

The new characteristics of Vaughan Williams's writing that confirmed themselves in *Job* were if anything more apparent in two of the major works whose composition immediately followed on from it, the Piano Concerto and the F Minor Symphony. He wrote the concerto sporadically from 1926 to 1931, again benefiting from the close attentions of Holst, and had begun the symphony by the start of 1932. According to his widow, he had the impulse to write it simply because of reading the account of the performance of another symphony in *The Times*. By the time of the F Minor's first performance in April 1935 Europe was well on course to a second and even more destructive war than the previous one, and it was felt that the composer had written a work that reflected the uncertainties and fears of the time. Vaughan Williams would always strongly reject the imputation of a programme to any of his symphonies that did not have one, and this would be the first such case. What is undeniable about the F Minor is that it reflects, whether consciously or unconsciously, contemporary life in the way that so little of

74

his music had done hitherto. While it is far from being the first example of great music written by him, it is outstanding because it is drawn so obviously from the world around him and not from any historical, biblical or mystical inspiration; the chains of folk-song had finally been shorn off.

Although the previous symphony, the *Pastoral*, had also concerned itself with war, that had been a real war. It had been written in its aftermath, and while the death and destruction soldiers like Vaughan Williams had witnessed were evoked in it, evoked all the more was the landscape in which those terrible things had happened. Looking back, it was a work of reflection; the F Minor, by contrast, looks forward, and is a work of terror – and very much sounds like it.

There had been, however, great prophecies of what was to come in the composer's style in the Piano Concerto, which he wrote for Harriet Cohen, whom he much admired. This work, which had been in gestation for so long, attracted little of the credit due to it when it was first performed in February 1933. It was an anti-sentimental concerto, remarkably unlike the recent work for the instrument of such composers as Rachmaninoff; yet it had passages of profound beauty and romanticism amidst stretches of percussive, aggressive writing that had, for many critics, too many unpleasant echoes of Busoni, a composer out of fashion then as now. If it has any contemporary cousins, then they are the two piano concertos of Vaughan Williams's old master, Ravel, and the work of Bartók.

For all the apparent debt to Busoni, the Vaughan Williams concerto is not so simply a derivative piece. It is the clearest sign yet that the composer was being increasingly influenced by a very contemporary force indeed – the 'Negroid emetics' of jazz – for the rhythms and cadences of that new music are all too apparent, not least in the last movement. By contrast, the second movement, a romanza, is of intense beauty, betraying both the composer's versatility and his growing ability to write romantic music in a modern style. Vaughan Williams, however, seems to have been depressed by the reception the concerto received, and almost disappointed in what he had done. He wrote to Boult, who conducted the first performance, that 'you have made impossible the composer's time-honoured excuse that the work would have sounded all right if it had been properly played. I could not have imagined a better performance.' The form of the work would, as we shall see, bother him for years to come. If it had a fault it was, unusually for this composer, that it was ahead of its time.

In the autumn of 1932, as he approached his sixtieth birthday, Vaughan Williams had made his second trip to America, this time without the increasingly immobile Adeline. He had spent much of the summer writing a series of lectures to be delivered at Bryn Mawr College, Pennsylvania, the theme of which – definitively for him – was 'National Music'. He passed the whole autumn term there, giving nine lectures in all, and found he and his music enjoyed what to him was a surprising degree of celebrity on the other side of the Atlantic. It is ironic that what would come to be interpreted as the authoritative statement of the Englishness of music – though the lectures were about national music applied to all nations – should have been

76

delivered in America, and with an American audience in mind. However, this undeniably made for greater clarity about the subject, since the lecturer knew he could take less for granted in some respects than had he been speaking to his own musical circle at home.

The lectures, as printed, begin with the declaration: 'Whistler used to say that it was as ridiculous to talk about national art as national chemistry. In saying this he failed to see the difference between art and science.' As the 'pure pursuit of knowledge', science knew no boundaries; art – especially the art of music – 'uses knowledge as a means to the evocation of personal experience in terms which will be intelligible to and command the sympathy of others. These others must clearly be primarily those who by race, tradition, and cultural experience are nearest to him.' It was precisely for this reason that Vaughan Williams's critics felt his music did not travel: though his supporters could point over the succeeding decades to performances of his music in concerts around the world, and the widespread availability and commercial success of his works on record, especially in America. His lack of cosmopolitanism was a problem only to some of his critics, not to him and not to his consistently expanding audience.

He condemned the man who had described music as 'the universal language'. 'It is not even true that music has an universal vocabulary, but even if it were so it is the use of the vocabulary that counts and no one supposes that French and English are the same language because they happen to use twenty-five out of twenty-six of the letters of the alphabet in common.' To support his thesis, he quoted Parry: 'True style comes not from the individual but from the products of crowds of fellow-workers who sift and try and try again till they have found the thing that suits their native taste . . . Style is ultimately national.' He compared the emergence of a national style in music in the preceding decades with the new, distinct style of buildings in America – 'when a stranger arrives in New York he finds imitations of Florentine palaces, replicas of Gothic cathedrals, suggestions of Greek temples, buildings put up before America began to realise that she had an artistic consciousness of her own.' By implication, he, Holst and the rest of their school were England's own musical consciousness, imitating no one. He explicitly rejected, however, any charge of artistic chauvinism. Making a call for a 'United States of the world' – and in doing so proving that the liberal optimism that had been born in him had not been entirely snuffed out by the Great War – he said that 'those will serve that universal state best who bring into the common fund something that they and they only can bring'.

Although he became homesick by the end of his two months away, the renewed experience of this brash, new country can only have had a positive effect on the development and pace of his creativity. As he became older, Vaughan Williams ran contrary to the type of his class and generation by becoming less conservative, less afraid of innovation, more willing to experiment. The divergence from the world of 'Linden Lea' with which he was still so associated could not have been greater: he wrote to his friend Maud Karpeles, the folk-song collector and scholar, from America to tell of 'a wonderful experience at the top of the "Empire State", first, sunset over the river and all the skyscrapers suddenly lighting up, then all the street lights came out and the moon. New York looked more classically and tragically beautiful than ever.'

It is to this modern world that the Piano Concerto, first performed shortly after his return, rightly belongs. That long gestation, from 1926, at the beginning of the new and more radical phase in his work and after *Sancta Civitas*, to 1930–31, had been for a very good reason. The concerto had remained unfinished for so long because he did not know how to finish it; and the end he eventually came up with did not satisfy him. It seemed to listeners sudden and somehow unresolved. Arnold Bax, on hearing it for the first time, told Herbert Howells that 'I don't think it is right formally at the end, for that last cadenza confuses the issue'; nevertheless, he said that 'I love that work of Ralph's and like it indeed better than anything else of his that I know.' It was a fiendishly difficult work to play: Vaughan Williams had no great sympathy for the piano, and in this respect only it shows.

When, by 1945, the piece for all its merits had failed to catch on he agreed to an arrangement by Joseph Cooper of the concerto for two pianos. There seem to have been doubts whether it was within the wit and skill of any contemporary pianist to play it as its composer had intended and, more to the point, to win the battle that the composer had designed the soloist to have with the orchestra. By having two pianos it was felt the orchestra would be put in its proper place. It was also at this time that he finally resolved his doubts about how the work should finish, and wrote a quiet ending to round off the piece on a note of calm and radiant beauty that looks back to the earlier romanza. It works brilliantly; though the two-piano version, sounding thick and at times clumsy, worked less so. It was not until, many years after the composer's death, when it was at last brilliantly recorded in the original version but with the revised ending, that it quickly took its place as one of the most sublime works ever written for the piano by an English composer, the forces of piano and orchestra in their correct balance at last and the emotions of the work properly resolved.

If the critics were puzzled, it was at least for the right reasons: that, at his relatively advanced age, Vaughan Williams was at last making his listeners think, and constantly surprising them. One critic, Frank Howes, wrote after the first performance of the Piano Concerto that the composer 'has a way of disconcerting his admirers with every new work of any size – there could be no more reassuring sign of artistic vigour and mental growth'. He was quite right; and there was much more of this to come. If the composer was worried about some of the incomprehension that now seemed routinely to accompany the emergence of each of his new major works, he had also decided not to let it deter him from continuing down his more radical path. The F Minor Symphony, to which Vaughan Williams now devoted himself for most of 1933, would be an even more provocative statement than the Piano Concerto.

He had an enforced holiday from writing during that summer, when he broke his leg and was unable to climb the stairs to his workroom at The White Gates. Suddenly at leisure, he tried and failed to learn the clarinet; by the end of August he was sufficiently recovered to be able to conduct his *Pastoral Symphony* at the Proms, and to fulfil another conducting engagement at the Three Choirs Festival at Hereford.

The next year would see a great change in the English musical landscape, and one that moved Vaughan Williams into what for the rest of his life would be his position as its unchallenged leading light. In February 1934, after years of relative silence and unwarranted neglect, and with only the sketches done for his third symphony, Elgar died, laden with honours like the establishment figure he was, and had so much wanted to be. For all their ideological and musical differences he and Vaughan Williams had great mutual respect, and it was a happy coincidence that, at the time of Elgar's death, his younger comrade should have been preparing a performance of *Gerontius* for the Leith Hill Festival. Over the years they had often met at the Three Choirs, which by the end of his life had almost become Elgar's personal festival; and Vaughan Williams had enjoyed teasing Elgar about religion and sharing bottles of beer with him.

Delius died a few weeks later; at his graveside Sir Thomas Beecham announced, *ex cathedra* as it were, that Vaughan Williams was now without question the leading figure in English musical life. This had nothing to do with Delius's death, but much to do with Elgar's. Beecham spoke of these matters with some objectivity: one of the numerous tales about him was that, having conducted a performance of *A Pastoral Symphony*, he proclaimed 'a city life for me!'

Of more personal concern to Vaughan Williams was the state of Holst's health. Though not yet sixty, his constitution had been undermined by a fall into the orchestra pit at

Reading a few years earlier. He had never enjoyed really good health, most recently having been debilitated by insomnia, an ulcer, gastric and blood disorders. In the winter of 1933–4 he was taken into a nursing home, where Vaughan Williams visited him whenever he was in London; he even took over temporarily some of Holst's duties at St Paul's School. A major operation to remove Holst's duodenal ulcer took place on 23 May 1934, but he was not nearly strong enough to stand a chance of surviving it, and died of heart failure two days later, three months after Elgar. Vaughan Williams was devastated; apart from George Butterworth, who was long gone, there had been no one else with whom he could have proper discussions about work in progress; and no one, musically, had ever been so close to him as Holst. He wrote to the composer's widow and daughter that 'my only thought is now which ever way I turn, what are we to do without him – everything seems to have turned back to him – what would Gustav think or advise or do . . .' Holst left his friend a tuning-fork, his prized possession: it had once belonged to Beethoven and had been given to Holst by an admirer.

The F Minor Symphony was the last work on which Holst would have any immediate influence. Vaughan Williams had written to him during his illness to say that, on his advice, he had expunged all the 'nice' tunes from the finale of the symphony, Holst having apparently succeeded in preventing his friend from undergoing a reversion to type. Yet the influence of Holst is to be heard in much of Vaughan Williams's writing over the following twenty-five years, and can be interpreted as reaching its peak in the Sixth Symphony; his effects were never entirely shaken off, and it was no bad thing they were not.

Vaughan Williams also became depressed about the worsening situation in Europe, watching Mussolini 'thundering at the door', as he told Maud Karpeles, and noting the growing tensions in Austria with a sense of foreboding. He was in bad spirits not just because of the loss of Holst, but also because he had cut the leg he had broken the previous year, and it had become poisoned. This laid him up for the best part of two months, further retarding his work. For all his denial of a programme for the symphony he was writing, it stretches credulity too far to believe that one as conscious as he was of what was happening abroad, and with such well-formed opinions on it (he complained to Maud Karpeles that 'the funny thing is that it seems to be our pacifist party in England who are crying out for us to intervene') could have kept it entirely separate from his music. Nor would it be too outrageous to imagine that the frustration the composer felt at having two enforced lay-offs from work because of his health were not in some way reflected in the anger and impatience of the new symphony.

He conducted at the Proms again that summer, though he was still so debilitated from his bad leg that he had to give the performance of *A London Symphony* and a new work based on folk-tunes, *The Running Set*, while sitting on a stool, to which he limped on a stick. This latter was in complete contrast to the violence of the incubating symphony, as was the other work of his to have a première that autumn, the *Suite for Viola* written for Lionel Tertis. Tertis, the leading violist of his time, had given the first performance of *Flos Campi*; this suite of eight pieces looks further back, being of that highly refined strain of English folk-music that was the essence of Vaughan Williams's idiom. It has, though, a sophistication and sadness that look forward five more years to the *Five Variants of Dives and Lazarus*, and (despite the occasional opportunity for virtuoso exhibitionism) is contemplative rather than simply picture-postcard; it is a greatly underrated work, both for its intrinsic beauty and its thoughtfulness.

The publication early in 1935 of the Bryn Mawr lectures as the book *National Music* was effectively the launch of Vaughan Williams's personal manifesto; and it should have been more comprehensible to his audience as a result of it that this man could be rooted in the indigenous music of England while turning out works more and more radical in their flavour. He was concentrating now on the last rehearsals for the first performance of the F Minor Symphony, given in London by Boult and the BBC Symphony Orchestra on 10 April 1935. William Walton, whose own symphony had just had its first performance, to massive and deserved acclaim, attended a rehearsal of the F Minor, and overheard Constant Lambert – not usually an admirer of Vaughan Williams – tell a fellow musician, Arthur Benjamin, that it was 'the greatest symphony since Beethoven'. Walton's own symphony had been ground-breaking, compelling, intense and exciting; but what Vaughan Williams had at last more than proved was that he could match these trends and qualities among the younger generation without being seen to imitate them. Although his voice had changed, it was still unmistakably his voice.

In the twenties, when Holst was the main point of comparison, Vaughan Williams had risked sounding staid and predictable next to his constantly innovative friend. Younger men besides Walton were making their mark. Bax, the leader of the generation after Vaughan Williams, was prolific and increasingly noticed. E.J. Moeran was holed up in County Kerry working on a symphony which, when first performed in 1938, would seem to owe much to Vaughan Williams and Sibelius but, at the same time, to have an idiom of its own and to be much more influenced by jazz even than Vaughan Williams was. Arthur Bliss would become celebrated in 1936 with his score for the film *Things to Come.* Benjamin Britten was in the first flush of his precocity, and would within the next few years produce a clutch of works of genius that represented a stunning departure for English music, notably the *Sinfonia da Requiem* and his Violin Concerto. Less well known, and now completely ostracised because of his eccentric extreme left-wing beliefs, John Foulds had written his masterpiece, the spectacular *Dynamic Triptych* for piano and orchestra, and gone off to India where he would die of cholera. This was a rich musical culture, rich beyond belief compared with the days when Parry, Stanford and Sir Arthur Sullivan were the only native composers of whom anyone had heard, when Elgar was struggling for acceptance, and when Vaughan Williams and Holst were immersed in their studies.

Boult's interpretation of the F Minor Symphony – which he later praised as 'a magnificent gesture of disgust' against the idea of war – by all accounts made the work. The violent, dissonant statement of musical belief that it constituted failed to surprise more only because of works such as *Job* and the

Piano Concerto, with their episodes of aggression, that had come before it. Even the unthinking majority who drank neat the accepted pastoral view of Vaughan Williams, and who had ignored the mounting evidence of the works of the preceding decade, had to accept that there could now be no more certainties about him as a composer. From the raging opening bars of the work until the thump that ends it just over half an hour later, it sounded as if the composer's mental blueprint had been torn up, and he had started instead from scratch.

He had always been individual; now, though, this was an individuality that drew its inspiration from the world about him, and not from some distant past. Some of his friends even suspected that his wife's increasing frailty and the realisation that she would never again be active were the main spurs to his anger, even more than the futility of war and international conflict. Typically, when asked what the F Minor Symphony was about, he allegedly replied: 'It is about F Minor.' The work seemed to scream out many things, not the least of which was its composer's pre-eminence in English musical life. To some it sounded discordant, perhaps the more so as a result of the expectations they might have had of this particular composer. The harsh sounds come so frequently and aggressively that they can only have been contrived, rather than having come about in Vaughan Williams's natural course of composition; they also hint at humour. In praising the work of another, less well-known composer who had been critically attacked for his discord, he made the point that such effects were justifiable if they were sincere: 'These discords come from a genuinely emotional impulse and not from a desire to outshine one's neighbour in hideosity.' Vaughan Williams himself was by no means trying to be competitive in writing a symphony of such violent and disturbing music; he wrote what he felt he had to write. 'I don't know whether I like it,' he said once it was completed, 'but it was what I meant.' He is also supposed to have said to an orchestra, having just conducted it, 'Gentlemen, if that is modern music, you can keep it.' Such remarks add to the suspicion that this was a gratuitous, forced, insincere exercise in modernism; yet on hearing the work, one knows at once that cannot be true.

As if to underline Vaughan Williams's new place at the head of the profession of music in England, King George V's private secretary wrote to him in May 1935 to invite him to join the Order of Merit. Having already declined a knighthood a few years earlier because it would have conflicted with his dislike of pomposity – and because, as he later said, 'I have always refused all honours and appointments which involved obligation to anyone in authority' – this latest offer caused him some anxiety. In the end, not least because the Order of Merit was of such high prestige (with just twenty-four members) and restricted to those of genuine eminence, and carried no obligations, he accepted the honour. He was also spurred to do so because the vacancy he would be filling had been created by the death of Elgar. As he saw it, he was to take up the place not just because of his own achievements but on behalf of the musical life of England, whose leader *de facto* he now was. He had already declined another honour left vacant by Elgar, the Mastership of the King's Musick, and would decline it again when Elgar's successor, Sir Walford Davies, died in 1941. The Order of Merit seemed to crown a career in music. It must have looked to the outside world that, at the age of sixty-three, Vaughan Williams would now start to wind down; but his best work was still to come, and more than half his symphonies had yet to be written.

If there was a growing preoccupation with the outside world – and it seems undeniable that there was – it was not allowed to affect Vaughan Williams's next major work, *Five Tudor Portraits*, a choral suite made of settings of five poems by John Skelton. The writing is by turns exuberant and sensuous, and is an exhibition piece of Vaughan Williams's art at the height of his powers. However antique the words might have been, the music is utterly modern, and with a definite swing to it; there are echoes, too, notably in the middle movement, 'John Jayberd', of Holst's *Choral Symphony*, which Vaughan Williams had found so difficult over a decade earlier when he had first heard it. Now, Holst's radicalism was taken up by his friend and admirer, and placed into the mainstream of the English choral tradition. There was a further debt in the inspiration; Elgar had suggested Skelton to Vaughan Williams some years earlier when they had met at a Three Choirs festival.

The *Portraits* have a great sense of humour about them, which perfectly echoes the sentiment of the poetry, but also a deep humanity. While they capture, on one level, the enthusiasm of the amateur choirs and music-makers whose recreation Vaughan Williams took so seriously, they also embody a suavity and self-assurance that say, perhaps more clearly than in any other work of his up to that date, that this was the pupil of Parry. They have much of Parry's self-confidence, a quality Vaughan Williams had long been able to express in his orchestral works but which seemed so often to have evaded him when writing choral pieces. While connecting as they do with the English choral tradition they also develop it and bring it up to date: so much so, in terms of the occasionally louche subject matter, that an elderly countess stalked out of the first performance claiming to have been shocked by what she heard. Yet, in including a drinking song, a love song, a lament, a satirical ballad and a depiction of a Tudor wide-boy, the suite also embodies many of the character traits from English life that have remained unchanged down the centuries.

In an even lighter vein he was working, too, on revising an operetta, *The Poisoned Kiss*, based on a short story he had read a few years earlier, and which he had written in the late twenties. Given the frustrations Vaughan Williams had had with his operas it is hard to understand why he went on, especially by experimenting with this variant of the genre; and this light musical comedy is by far the least satisfactory of his works for the musical stage. It was not the sort of thing for which audiences were primed in the nineteen thirties, and its day has yet to come. It was met with indifference after its first performance in May 1936, and the composer did not help with the tone of his programme note: 'The audience is requested *not* to refrain from talking during the overture. Otherwise they will know all the tunes before the opera begins.' As with *Hugh*, it was not the music that was the problem – though it was of a lightness that caused many critics to fail to be able to take it very seriously – but the libretto that was the work's real undoing.

He could take some comfort, however, from the realisation at last of his short one-act opera *Riders to the Sea*: although, as Michael Kennedy points out, the composer does not refer to the work as an opera, merely the setting to music of Synge's play of the same name. At least, by taking this course, Vaughan Williams would have no problems with the libretto; and from the moment the work opens the listener is struck by the suitability of the mournful, reflective music to a text that deals with death, poverty and the subordination of man to nature in the west of Ireland. It seems a short step from a setting such as this, especially in the balance of music and voices, to the operatic achievements of Benjamin Britten less than a decade later, from *Peter Grimes* onwards. What *Riders* has in common with the operatic works of Britten is that, as in those works, the emotion is profound and the characters three-dimensional. Thanks to his choice of libretto, Vaughan Williams was at last able to be regarded with the seriousness that his musical talent should anyway have demanded.

The score of the opera was published in 1936, and it had its first performance in 1937. Its length – just thirty-five minutes – has militated against its being produced more than very occasionally, which, rather than the quality of the work, has led to its neglect. Sadly, Vaughan Williams's general operatic reputation may have gone before him in this matter too, not least when the most recent manifestation of it had been *The Poisoned Kiss*. If only he could have found a serious theme like *Riders*, and extended it over two or three acts, he might have altered that perception of his talents in this department. He believed, of course, that he had found such a theme – *The Pilgrim's Progress* – but after thirty years of thought and occasional work on it, he was no nearer, as he saw it, making that most English of texts into an opera.

Riders has an idiom consistent with what was now the main burden of Vaughan Williams's creativity. So, too, does the cantata *Dona Nobis Pacem*, on which he worked during the winter of 1935–6. There is no concealing here the composer's agitation with international events. His starting point was a sombre setting he had made a quarter of a century earlier, but never published, of Whitman's 'Dirge for Two Veterans'. He added two more Whitman poems, some words from the Bible and, most inspired of all, words from John Bright's speech to the House of Commons on 23 February 1855 lamenting the effects of the war in the Crimea. Although the work is marked by the nobility typical of Vaughan Williams's writing, which puts him firmly in the same culture as Elgar for all their other artistic differences, it also expresses an anguish and a regret not heard before in his music, even in *Sancta Civitas* – which, though similar in outlook, is by comparison a more passive work – and the F Minor Symphony of the previous year. The cantata is so strikingly vivid partly as a result of this greater injection of emotion.

The tone of lamentation is set from the moment of the pained cry from the orchestra that introduces the work, preparing us for the soprano's unusually passionate rendition of the 'Agnus Dei'. If the F Minor Symphony introduced Vaughan Williams as a man of more complex emotions than had hitherto been suspected, *Dona Nobis Pacem* confirms it; as it confirms that this is now a composer whose main inspiration is drawn not from the soil of England, but from the whole world going mad around him. Vaughan Williams was no appeaser; he was disgusted by what he saw and heard of what was happening in Germany. *Dona Nobis Pacem* is not a cry for peace at any price; it is a pre-emptive lament for the fact that there may well have to be another war, and for the suffering that will have to be caused before certain elements come to their senses. There are moments of optimism in the 'Gloria' that comes towards the end of the work, but the predominant tone of sadness in the words of the soprano, who returns to sing, uneasily, 'Dona Nobis Pacem' at the end, sets the tone of the work. Other words the composer has set – 'Nation shall not lift up a sword against nation, neither shall they learn war any more' – sound more like a plea than a complacent expression of fact.

It is arrestingly dramatic music, the more so because one instinctively senses that there was nothing remotely affected in the emotions that provoked Vaughan Williams to write it. He had never been anything other than a sincere composer; now his sincerity connected with a wider audience of his fellow Britons, for his concerns and theirs were becoming identical: something he might have regarded as a necessary component of a national music, and why his music was now truly 'ultimately national'. In the years leading up to the war this fact would seem to have been underlined by the frequency with which festivals and concert arrangers programmed *Dona Nobis Pacem*, often with the composer conducting: he had caught, with unerring accuracy, the mood of the times, and it had given his music a new lease of life.

With first performances of this new cantata, of *Five Tudor Portraits* and of *The Poisoned Kiss*, 1936 was a year of great and diverse achievement for Vaughan Williams. In January 1937 the *Times* music critic, commenting on the first London performance of *Five Tudor Portraits*, wrote that the composer's recent works 'have created the impression that while Vaughan Williams's tone of voice is recognisable among living composers, one never knows what he will be at next'. This was true, and would further be proved to be so; but what is easier to see at this remove than it was then is that the predominant tone of voice was changing. This would be true even of his next symphony, his fifth, which he began to contemplate towards the end of 1937 as he passed his sixty-fifth birthday. He had started to convince himself that, after all, he would never write his long-projected opera about *The Pilgrim's Progress*, and resolved to use some of the music he had sketched for it in a symphony inspired by the idea. When it came, though, it would not be conventional pastorality, or even the war-ravaged image of it conveyed by *A Pastoral Symphony*; it would take a much more imaginative approach to these mystical ideas, and even in the midst of the most beautiful passages the symphony would betray a strong underlying tension.

Vaughan Williams was soon presented with an opportunity to make clear his revulsion at what was happening in Germany. Although he accepted a prize for conspicuous achievement in the arts awarded by the University of Hamburg in the summer of 1937 – a sign that his music was attracting a growing audience abroad in a way that only Elgar's, of all modern British composers', had hitherto done – he did so with great reservations. He was sensible of the great honour that the prize did not so much to him as to English music, which the Germans especially had always considered something of a poor relation. He believed that, were he to accept, his music and other music of the English school would become better known and appreciated in Europe. However, as he wrote in a note to himself at the time, 'I am strongly opposed to the present system of government in Germany, especially with regard to its treatment of artists and scholars. I belong to more than one English society whose object is to combat all that the present German regime stands for. Therefore am I the kind of person to whom a German University would wish to offer a prize?'

He did accept: though to reconcile this act with his conscience he confirmed in his letter of acceptance that the university had stated that the honour 'implies no political propaganda and that I shall feel free as an honourable man, if I accept, to hold and express any views on the general state of Germany which are allowable to any British citizen.' The fact that Vaughan Williams was a supporter of various committees pledged to work against Nazism and to help refugees from Nazi persecution led, within eighteen months of his accepting this honour, to his music being placed on a blacklist in the Third Reich; which proved the very point he had long been making about the stupidity and evil of the regime. His hopes that, by accepting, he would be leading a great act of evangelism for English music in Europe's most powerful country and most distinguished musical culture were dashed by a level of prejudice and wickedness that even he, it seems, had not been able to envisage as being possible.

After the great burst of creativity he had enjoyed during the mid-thirties, he soon found that the wheel had turned again, and that it was proving harder and harder to get down to composition. His recent heavy output had been matched with a still extensive workload at the RCM, as well as regular conducting engagements in London and at various festivals. His wife was now seriously disabled, mostly housebound, and had withdrawn greatly into herself. Although he had many close and devoted friends, Vaughan Williams was more alone, in some respects, than he had ever been. Holst's death had robbed him of his closest and most trusted musical friend; and while Adeline still provided a discerning and intelligent court of opinion, the two of them inevitably came to lead increasingly separate lives. He told a colleague in the winter of 1937–8 that 'I feel absolutely dried up at present and have the feeling that I shall never write another note of music.' Soon a commission arrived that would give the lie to these claims of creative impotence. Sir Henry Wood, founder of the Promenade Concerts, was celebrating fifty years in music, and asked for a setting of lines from *The Merchant of Venice* for sixteen soloists, eight male and eight female. The result was the *Serenade to Music*, first performed on 5 October 1938 and, famously, recorded the following day with the same team of soloists, all of whom had worked regularly with Wood. It is a magical and appropriately serene piece, art for the sake of art, a work of poise, sensuality and great beauty.

During 1938 and early 1939 Vaughan Williams worked on

music for a masque, *The Bridal Day*, based on the poem 'Epithalamion' by Edmund Spenser, Shakespeare's near-contemporary. The words had been arranged by Ursula Wood, a young woman who had written to Vaughan Williams with the idea some months earlier, and whom he had been prevailed upon to meet. Just twenty-seven, she was the wife of a regular soldier and had trained for the stage. Having until a few years previously had no interest in music, that had all been changed in a moment of revelation, when she witnessed an early performance of *Job*. Vaughan Williams, almost forty years her senior, and Mrs Wood hit it off immediately. Gentle, unstuffy, generous and amusing, he had a natural affinity with younger people of both sexes, to whom he was 'Uncle Ralph'. As well as collaborating with him on *The Bridal Day*, Mrs Wood started to help him with other tasks, such as typing out and editing the libretto for another opera he was planning, but never realised, on the Belshazzar theme. She soon became a regular companion. *The Bridal Day* reached the point, by the spring of 1939, of having a play-through by a quartet supplemented with piano and flute, with the composer singing the baritone part. Such play-throughs, in front of a 'jury' of friends whose judgement Vaughan Williams trusted, had become a substitute for the scrutiny of his work by Holst: there was no one else left whom he could trust to understand and sympathise with what he was trying to do, and whom he felt able to consult while in the midst of creation.

Six

The Importance of War

The realisation of *The Bridal Day*, intended for later in 1939, was prevented by the outbreak of war. It was put to one side, and had to wait until long after the war was over before it could be performed. Once war was declared, against an enemy Vaughan Williams had long since identified as evil, he threw himself into the effort against Hitler. At sixty-seven he could not respond as he had in 1914. This time his contribution was made by taking in evacuees, collecting salvage, helping with the war savings campaign, giving over some of his land for allotments, and trying to find work for refugees. He became a fanatical gardener, growing mountains of vegetables, and started to keep chickens. He had always liked his food – his dying at so great an age was a standing rebuke to those who claim that such indulgence is a sure route to an early grave – and was determined that he and his would not go hungry, whatever Hitler might do to them.

In artistic matters, he recognised the usefulness of music in maintaining morale, and was one of those behind the idea and execution of Dame Myra Hess's lunchtime concerts at the National Gallery in London. It was appropriate that, in this time of great national peril, the next of his works to be given a first British performance was his *Five Variants of Dives and Lazarus*, a short work for string orchestra and harp based on one of England's oldest folk-tunes, the one the composer claimed that, on first hearing it, the listener felt he had known all his life. It is a musical symbol of the continuity and values of England. Although it consciously looked back – 'these variants', the composer wrote, 'are not exact replicas of traditional tunes, but rather reminiscences of various versions in my own collection and those of others' – the work was also designed as a statement to the world of the health and fortitude of the English musical renaissance. The composer's earlier orchestral treatments of folk-songs had been quite literal, almost superficial; this is more reflective, tempered not just by a great experience of composition and by a still abundant facility for invention, but also by the realities of a violent and insecure world from which there was an increasing need to seek some form of refuge. In this sense it is the precursor of the E major section of the Sixth Symphony, the one brief moment of escape in that darkest and most martial of works.

Dives and Lazarus was an explicit advertisement for the 'national music', commissioned as it had been for the World's Fair in New York. Its first performance was given in Carnegie Hall in June 1939, and by the time the conductor on that occasion, Adrian Boult, gave the first British performance in Bristol in November 1939 the world had undergone another of its periodic lurches into grave uncertainty. In such a context the retrospection of the piece is no act of indulgence, but rather an affirmation of the civilisation for which Vaughan Williams's fellow Britons were now fighting. He saw war, when it came, as all the more reason to make music. In a controversial article on the role of the composer in wartime, he wrote:

It is right even to learn from the enemy. There has been in Germany of late years a 'Home Music' movement. Some of the best-known composers have occupied their time and their talents in arranging and composing music for the amateur to play in his own home, I should like to see this idea developed here – music for every fortuitous combination of instruments which may happen to be assembled in a parlour or a dug-out, with a part for anyone who happens to drop in.

This was a war between civilisation and no civilisation; and the national consciousness that would be needed for Britain to survive and to win it could, the composer knew, be harnessed by just the common culture for which he had been evangelising for the previous forty years.

As he was not occupied on active service, there would be no repeat of the hiatus in his creative life that had occurred during the Great War. His first project was to set some lines of Shelley's from *Prometheus Unbound*, a project in which he enlisted Ursula Wood, and which would be completed as *Six Choral Songs*. Once the initial shock of the wartime emergency wore off more performances of music were possible. Having at first imagined there would be no opportunity for any sort of Leith Hill festival, Vaughan Williams and the committee organised performances in March 1940 of *Elijah* and *Judas*

Maccabeus, precisely the sort of music banned by the Jew-hating Nazis in Germany. Shortly afterwards he conducted his *Mass in G Minor* at St Paul's Cathedral. The mounting loss of life, as the 'phoney war' came to an end in the spring of 1940, distressed him; and like many political radicals at the time he became an enthusiast for the idea, once the war was over, of a federal European union to prevent, as they saw it, any such war happening again.

Meanwhile, he dug an air-raid shelter at The White Gates and sandbagged the house; the Battle of Britain would shortly take place in the skies above the Home Counties. In September 1940, on the day before the anniversary of the declaration of war, its reality was brought directly home to them: Honorine Williamson, a niece of Adeline Vaughan Williams's sister who had lived at The White Gates, and before that at Cheyne Walk, for twelve years as a companion to Adeline and *de facto* daughter to both of them, was killed in an air-raid in London.

Having longed for some constructive official war work, Vaughan Williams was in 1940 appointed chairman of a Home Office committee considering the release of interned alien musicians, many of whom, as Jews or anti-Nazis, had fled Germany before the war only to find themselves under suspicion now as fears of invasion and fifth columnists mounted. Here, too, Vaughan Williams had a close personal interest. He had met a refugee German composer, Robert Müller-Hartmann, through Imogen Holst, daughter of his late friend. Müller-Hartmann was released from internment in the spring of 1941 and came to live near Vaughan Williams in Dorking, with some mutual friends. He and the composer became close, to the extent that Vaughan Williams would discuss with him problems in his own work in a way he had done with no one since Holst's death. The sombre mood he felt at that early stage of the war, when invasion and the destruction of his way of life were daily threatened, is clearly reflected in the piece he wrote at the time, the motet *Valiant for Truth*, another manifestation of his continuing obsession with Bunyan and written after the death of an old and close friend, Dorothy Longman. For all the uncertainty and darkness of the times, the climax – 'and the trumpets sounded for him on the other side' – shows that this agnostic still had some need for hope, and expectation that it might be fulfilled.

The war brought an exciting new departure for Vaughan Williams, and one that would influence his musical output for the rest of his life. One of his former pupils, Muir Mathieson, had made a big name for himself in the film world. He commissioned his old teacher to write the music for a Powell and Pressburger film, *49th Parallel*. It was a high-quality production, and one whose ethical values will strongly have appealed to Vaughan Williams. Michael Powell and Emeric Pressburger – the latter a Jewish refugee from eastern Europe – had long been committed anti-Nazis, like Vaughan Williams, and their story depicted fanatical Nazi evil, and how justice eventually triumphs over it. The film included some of the leading actors of the day, including Laurence Olivier, Leslie Howard and Eric Portman, and was a thinly-disguised plea for the Americans to come into the war against Germany. Although he had to work quickly, since the film was already in production, and had to write to split-second timings, he flourished under these new disciplines. His film music, for this and for others, remains among the finest ever written. Echoes of it would occur in his other works, and there is a cinematic quality to much of his music in the forties and fifties, whether written for the cinema or not. As can be heard when listening to the scores of most British films of the period, a whole school of British composers for the cinema came to owe either a conscious or unconscious debt to Vaughan Williams's writing for this medium. When *49th Parallel* was released in the autumn of 1941 it provoked several other commissions for film music, which he readily accepted, beginning with *Coastal Command* for the Crown Film Unit. There would, in all, be eleven such scores.

He then moved on to write his second string quartet, thirty-five years after its predecessor, and some variations of Welsh hymn tunes that he entitled *Household Music*. By early 1942 his committee work had mushroomed, notably to include the Council for the Encouragement of Music and the Arts, which would become the Arts Council. The Vaughan Williamses also took in, for a time, Ursula Wood, whose soldier husband died not at the front but, ironically, of a heart attack at a very early age. She would share the composer's study and work at her poetry and other writing while he wrestled with his work at the other side of the room, at this stage the music for a new feature film, *Flemish Farm*.

A measure of Vaughan Williams's stature in national and musical life came with the extent of the commemorations of his seventieth birthday in October 1942. A special concert was given at the National Gallery on the day itself; there were broadcasts of his music, and Gerald Finzi, for whom

Vaughan Williams had the highest regard among the younger generation of composers, dedicated to him his Shakespeare song-cycle, *Let Us Garlands Bring*. Even a composer who had been scorchingly critical of Vaughan Williams, Constant Lambert, dedicated a new work to him on this special occasion, the *Aubade Héroique* – 'a fact which, to be quite frank, is relished by neither of us', as Lambert put it to a friend. The festivities peaked with the composer conducting *Dona Nobis Pacem* and *A Sea Symphony* at the Royal Albert Hall in early November. If some felt that reaching three-score-and-ten would mark a winding down in his creative life, one who knew him well offered an alternative and, as it turned out, more accurate view. His cousin Ralph Wedgwood told him, 'the last Rembrandts were the best, the last Titians the most surprising'. Another old friend, George Trevelyan, now Master of Trinity, spoke of the 'national outburst of feeling' that the birthday had provoked. Vaughan Williams had become what would now be called an icon, a living representative of a quality that the English recognised as special and important to them, and who communicated directly with them. While this did not stop younger men sniping at him on account of the idiom in which he wrote, and at what they thought was the prejudice against continental influences that he embodied, by the integrity of his music and the strength of his character he none the less commanded their respect.

Once the celebrations were over he moved into the final phase of work on his Fifth Symphony, the composition that would further convince his public that he had finally entered some sort of creative departure lounge. By the end of January

1943 he had made a two-piano version of the work, which was played through by two pianist friends near his home in Surrey. According to his widow, he was beset by doubts about the new symphony, his mood not helped by an accident Adeline had on returning home from the play-through, when she twisted her foot. It had its first orchestral play-through by the London Philharmonic in Maida Vale on 25 May 1943, an exercise that greatly reassured the composer as to its quality. He himself conducted the first performance at a Prom on 24 June, and it was broadcast by the BBC as a great national event, which in cultural terms it was. Still in the midst of war – though in the relative lull London experienced between the end of the Blitz and the coming of the V-1s, and in the period of elation that grew out of the victory over Rommel in the Western Desert the previous November – its serenity seemed like an earnest of the peace to come. In a typically modest gesture to another great composer, Vaughan Williams dedicated the symphony 'to Jean Sibelius, without permission'.

It is one of the paradoxes of Vaughan Williams's art that this apparently escapist work should have been heard in wartime, while his most violent and martial should have marked the years of peace that followed it. Since, however, it took as its inspiration a theme the composer had been contemplating for much of his adult life – *The Pilgrim's Progress* – it is no wonder the symphony has the flavour it does: that it emerged in wartime was not for it to be a prediction of peace, but merely as an accident of birth. The work represents a new high-point in Vaughan Williams's skills of orchestration and musical invention. Though apparently

celestial in its conception, it none-the-less embodies at different times tension, humour, sadness, leading up to a resolution
that sounds like a benediction. It has definite antecedents –
notably the Lento and Epilogue of the *London Symphony* – but
at the same time it is clear to see in retrospect how it was the
natural and inevitable intellectual predecessor to the Sixth,
even though the two symphonies could hardly be more
different.

When the Committee for the Promotion of New Music was
formed in January 1943, Vaughan Williams accepted its
presidency. Most obviously as a teacher, he had always
helped younger composers to fulfil their talents. Butterworth
was the first, Moeran was encouraged by him and, later,
Finzi became much admired. His regard for and willingness
to help younger composers was not in the least sectarian; he
went to great lengths, though unsuccessfully, to prevent
Michael Tippett – whose music was quite unlike Vaughan
Williams's and whose pacifist political views he fundamentally disagreed with – from being sent to prison when, as a
conscientious objector, he refused to take agricultural work.
Tippett was teaching at Morley College, the working men's
establishment in South London where Holst had conducted
musical studies for years, and Vaughan Williams felt that his
involvement in keeping musical life going was just as important for the war effort as what the government thought he
should be doing. The CPNM helped ensure that new music
had first performances, thereby giving encouragement to
younger composers to persist in their vocation. That there
was now so much competition to have works performed was
itself a tribute to the renaissance in English musical life that

Parry and Stanford can be credited with having started, and which Elgar, Vaughan Williams and Holst in their different ways brought to fruition.

With the Fifth Symphony successfully launched, Vaughan Williams's next work was an Oboe Concerto for Leon Goossens – a piece that owes much to the symphony that preceded it, having grown out of a discarded scherzo. This occupied him well into 1944, much of which was spent arranging for the transfer of his childhood home, Leith Hill Place, to the National Trust. Vaughan Williams's mother had lived there until her death in 1937 at the age of ninety-five, and he had subsequently inherited the house from his brother Hervey in May 1944. On the very day of Hervey's death he went to see James Lees-Milne at the Trust's head-quarters to announce his decision to get the property off his hands. Lees-Milne did not realise until Vaughan Williams had left that he was the composer, though he found him 'an elderly, stout man, handsome and distinguished, not at all practical'. When Lees-Milne went, a fortnight later, to visit the property he noted in his diary that,

> the composer is a very sweet man, with a most impressive appearance. He is big and broad and has a large head with sharply defined features, and eyes that look far into the distance . . . in the car he told me that when young musicians came to him for advice he always discouraged them, for he said that those who seriously intended to make music their career would always do so willy-nilly. He has a quiet, dry humour which expresses itself in very few words. He laughs in a low key.

During 1944 Vaughan Williams put the finishing touches to his second string quartet, and started to contemplate a new and radically different symphony. That was a work directly influenced by the war; but before it was too far advanced it seemed that the war itself would be over. The BBC, in expectation of this event, asked him in September 1944 to write a piece in thanksgiving for the country's deliverance from Nazism, which became *A Thanksgiving for Victory*, and for which he chose lines from *Henry V*. There was more than just national survival on Vaughan Williams's mind that autumn; his wife, now seventy-five, caught a cold that developed into pneumonia and pleurisy, and he feared she would die: she recovered, but her health was now gravely weak. She had been unable to walk since the injury to her foot in January 1943.

The *Thanksgiving* was recorded by the BBC in November 1944, and held for broadcast on the first Sunday after the expected victory; which, though delayed beyond what were the original expectations of the country, finally came in May 1945. That winter he worked slowly at his Sixth Symphony, and more thoroughly at the apparently interminable project of writing his opera based on *The Pilgrim's Progress*. In 1942 he had written music for a BBC production of the morality, and its success had persuaded him that, even though he had used some of his musical ideas for his last symphony, the project was worth persisting with. His widow has described the composer's routine at this time: up by six for an hour and a half's work before breakfast, then another session from nine until lunch at 12.30; only a little more work would be done in the afternoon, with possibly a session after supper if there was nothing on the wireless to which he wanted to listen. Though seventy-two when the war ended, he was in infinitely more robust condition than his afflicted wife, the result partly of an iron constitution, but also of continuous activity – whether gardening or charging around on his musical and administrative work. It is a vigour that amply comes over in the symphony on which he was working, which could not sound less like an old man's music.

He was much occupied too with writing for films. His success in the genre had led to his being taken up by Ealing Studios, for whom he was writing a score for *The Loves of Joanna Godden*, a film about a woman in Victorian England running a farm on Romney Marsh. Some themes left over from the score he had written for his last big feature film, the war story *Flemish Farm*, would find their way into the Sixth Symphony, further reinforcing the point that his writing for the cinema was never an end in itself. Sadler's Wells decided to put on *Sir John in Love* – its first professional performance – and the composer immediately set to revising it. Revision of his scores was one of his principal vices: he rarely believed a piece of music was 'finished'. However, the long-awaited opportunity to have one of his operas put on by a professional company clearly called for him to cast more than a casual eye over the score.

For all these diversions, the Sixth Symphony was now at an advanced stage. In the summer of 1946 he invited a few close friends – including Adrian Boult, who would conduct its first performance, Gerald Finzi and his wife, and Ursula Wood, who still spent a great deal of time at The White Gates – to his home to hear the pianist Michael Mullinar play through the symphony on the piano. The brilliance with which Mullinar realised the composer's vision with such limited forces led Vaughan Williams to dedicate the work to him; the impact on those who heard this first flowering on that summer's day was indicative of the seismic effect the completed symphony would have on British musical life when it came upon the public less than two years later. The composer himself was, according to his widow, much less affected by self-doubt about the symphony than he had been by previous major works. 'Ralph was very lively and chatty about it,' she recalled, his exuberance stimulated by the immediately enthusiastic response of those who had heard it.

With the end of the war there had been an upsurge in musical performances in London. Vaughan Williams conducted three of his five symphonies at the Proms that summer and, as if such work did not occupy him enough, set about forming a Bach choir in Dorking. In the winter of 1947 Sadler's Wells continued their patronage of him, and put on *The Shepherds of the Delectable Mountains*. Although he had been remarkably confident about his new symphony after Mullinar's realisation of it he had revised the score, and was anxiously awaiting a further play-through by the pianist in March 1947. However, a new bout of illness for his wife, and an increasing schedule not just of rehearsals but also of recording, meant the day had to be postponed until June. His brother-in-law R.O. Morris, who attended the play-through at the RCM, wrote to Adeline Vaughan Williams to say that 'the sustained vigour and originality of the musical idea is most imposing'. Morris's perception was acute: the key to the shock of this symphony was that its musical force was relentless, and it had an atmosphere and a structure without precedent in the composer's canon.

Vaughan Williams seemed to be happier once he had heard this latest play-through, and a first performance was set for April 1948. The work was played through again at the BBC's Maida Vale studios in December 1947, in the form that it would take at its first performance – the composer having, as was his habit, made several adjustments in the preceding six months – and with Adrian Boult, who would have the first performance, taking turns with the composer to conduct the music. Robert Müller-Hartmann was among those invited to hear it, and was plunged into such an emotional state by it that he left the studios suddenly rather than reveal himself as too overcome to speak to the composer. He too had heard it before on the piano, but 'I never anticipated the overwhelming impression the real thing would make on me', as he subsequently wrote to the composer.

Once the symphony was completed Vaughan Williams returned to an unsuccessful work of the immediate pre-war years, his *Double Trio*, which he had withdrawn in 1939 shortly after its first performance and then revised during the war. It has an important link with the Sixth Symphony not just in chronology, but in its musical language. The Sixth is infused with the rhythms of jazz; so too is the work that was made out of the *Double Trio*, the *Partita for Double String Orchestra*, which had its first performance in March 1948, a month before the new symphony. Its third movement is entitled *Homage to Henry Hall*, in tribute to the celebrated leader of the BBC's dance orchestra. Hall's theme tune,

'Here's to the Next Time', is in fact merely the basis of the movement in his homage, but is dealt with even more radically and extensively in the preceding movement.

Some critics have expressed surprise that Vaughan Williams should have admired Hall, but that is to see only one obvious facet of the composer's character. It is also to fail to understand the increasingly contemporary nature of his writing as he approached old age, and the effect upon him of the fast-changing world. This is sophisticated, sensuous music of experience and of its time; it serves as the perfect prelude to the symphony that so shortly followed it. There are stark contrasts in tone between the first three movements, with their almost louche atmosphere, which were developed from the *Double Trio*, and the intense, conflict-laden finale that proves itself an exact contemporary of the symphony. As he became older and his handwriting deteriorated from its already parlous state, Vaughan Williams used other musicians to help clean up – or as he put it, 'wash the face' of – his scores. The *Partita* was 'washed' by Müller-Hartmann, to whom it is dedicated.

Within three days during the previous October the Vaughan Williamses celebrated their fiftieth wedding anniversary, and he his seventy-fifth birthday, which was marked by tribute and broadcast concerts in London and in Dorking. In a wireless talk Boult, himself a musical figure of great authority, called him 'the undisputed leader of English musical life'. He reflected upon how the development of Vaughan Williams's musical language was identical in many respects to that of English musical language as a whole; and how it might well be at times incomprehensible to foreign ears. If this was so, it was not just because of the self-consciousness with which Vaughan Williams, along with Holst and followed by Butterworth, had made themselves 'English' composers, rather than settle for being offshoots of the German tradition. It was also because the English experience by which Vaughan Williams was now inspired was not simply rooted in the past and in the soil, but came from the fact of living in England and seeing England prevail through times of great crisis, fear and destruction. This was a tellingly accurate judgement, but then Boult knew more than most about the tenor of the work in progress.

At about this time Vaughan Williams not only wrote the music for a short film, but also took part in it. Now largely forgotten, *The Dim Little Island* was made for the Central Office of Information by one of the great lost geniuses of the English cinema, Humphrey Jennings, and was meant as benign propaganda during a time of austerity and shaky national self-confidence. Together with three other men – a shipbuilder, a naturalist and the cartoonist Osbert Lancaster – Vaughan Williams read a commentary about a facet of British national life that should give everyone cause to believe that the British people, in the words of one of the other speakers, had not 'lost it as a nation'. The composer's contribution, other than his arrangement of *Dives and Lazarus* as the film's score, is about the cohesion of a common culture and, naturally, the part music plays in it. He harks back to *Dives and Lazarus* – the use of which in a film like this, about harnessing a national spirit, could not have been more appropriate – and how folk-song is the birthright of every Englishman and national music (not a phrase he uses, but it is implicit in all he says) is a vital and precious resource.

As *Dives* plays, the composer says: 'Listen to that tune. It is one of our English folk-tunes. I knew it first when I was quite a small boy, but I realised even then that here was something not only very beautiful, but which had a special appeal to me as an Englishman.' It is one of 'those great tunes, which like our language, our customs, our laws are the groundwork upon which everything must stand'. He praised those who were 'spreading the knowledge and love of music', and referred to the 'late war' as a 'great upheaval of national consciousness and emotion' that should inspire musicians, performers, composers, but also those who simply wanted to listen and to appreciate. What he has to say is about music as a means of creating a common national spirit, and of communing with that national spirit: it is his idea of music being one of the things that people in a nation have in common, for it represents their shared experiences. On a sentimental, atavistic level a tune like *Dives* did just that; but so, too, would his next symphony, in ways at the same time similar and very different.

At last, some of the infirmities of age were catching up with him: most distressingly deafness, which affected his ability to hear very high and very low notes. He also found his new symphony difficult to conduct at the first orchestral play-through in Maida Vale that December – though it was generally agreed that his conducting had been somewhat problematical for some time – and in hearing it in its proper form for the first time he made more minor changes to the score. Though he was not to know it at the time, the germ for a seventh symphony was about to arrive. Ernest Irving, the director of music at Ealing Studios, had after much lobbying succeeded in persuading Vaughan Williams to write a score for the forthcoming film *Scott of the Antarctic*. Once he began work on the idea he found it gripped him, and it occupied him for much of 1948.

The Sixth Symphony had its first performance on 21 April 1948 in the Albert Hall. The effect it had was of a detonation; there was nothing in what Vaughan Williams had done before to prepare his audience, in the hall and listening to a relay on the wireless, for what they heard. One critic, Scott Goddard, said that the symphony was addressed to 'that immortal force, the spirit of man'. As Michael Kennedy, who was a young man at the time, wrote later in relation to that comment: 'In the troubled and turbulent post-war world the music penetrated to that spirit as neither of its two predecessors had fully done, whatever their musical virtues.' The assault – there is no other word for it – of the opening bars of the Sixth utterly destroyed the notion, prevalent after the Fifth, that that last symphony had been a signing-off, or a pronouncement that the composer's musical language had been finally settled as having its main point of reference in pastorality and a benign mysticism. Its impact was, as the symphony's most perceptive critic, Deryck Cooke, put it, 'violently emotional', the effect on him at the first performance 'nothing short of cataclysmic'.

Its roots may be discerned in *Job*, or the Fourth Symphony, or in some of the film music of the war years; for these were the earlier proofs of changes in the composer's musical language away from the pastoral or the modal. It is Vaughan

Williams's most Holstian piece of music; had his friend lived, one can be sure there would have been no failure of comprehension on his part about what the composer was trying to do, nor, one suspects, much criticism of how he was trying to do it. What it most has in common with Holst is an ability to chill and to warm almost in successive bars; which in itself assists the creation of a feeling of turmoil. There is also, in the first movement especially, a clarity of expression and a smoothness of writing that creates the most vivid emotional effects, just as Holst had so often done from *The Planets* onwards; the most direct ancestor of the E major section in the first movement is the grand tune in *Jupiter*.

The rage enunciated in the Fourth Symphony is musically, but not always emotionally, coherent. In the Sixth it is both, and in that respect the work is the natural successor to the beautifully crafted Fifth. The Fourth displays a self-consciousness in its brutality; the Sixth does not. It is, instead, a natural and naturally articulate expression of feeling, so different from all that had preceded it as to be at times unrecognisable as a work of this composer. For all the super-ficial similarities between elements of the Fourth and Sixth symphonies, Vaughan Williams was speaking what was for him a completely new language. If it has antecedents, they are the First Symphony of Walton, the Symphony in G of Moeran, or the *Sinfonia da Requiem* of Britten, all from the preceding decade or so; and further afield, the work of Shostakovich. The music of the first movement is restless, violent, aggressive, dark and hypnotic. There is jauntiness and humour, both characteristics expressed through the debt to jazz. The syncopation that infuses the first movement returns in the scherzo in a more savage form, locating the work exactly in its time.

There is a relentlessness to the music that both spellbinds and batters, exacerbated by the fact that the four movements are played without a break. Significantly, it also has an effect that is clearly cinematic, especially in the E major section, and which is of the same tone as the lush and overtly romantic theme music to *49th Parallel*. It is this part of the work that provides the clearest intellectual link with the rest of Vaughan Williams's music: it assures us that, for all its radicalism, the Sixth is nothing if not a very English work, written at a time of heightened national consciousness, and in part a search for something familiar and 'rooted in the soil of England'. That, more than its inventiveness and experimentalism, explains the peculiar appeal it had to English audiences at the time. This was, as the composer had said in his 1932 lectures, the use of a common knowledge 'as a means to the evocation of personal experience' to others 'primarily those who by race, tradition, and cultural experience are the nearest to him; in fact . . . his own nation'. If this symphony has a blueprint, it is to be found in those words; and the work would have an astonishing success partly because it evoked the common cultural experience Vaughan Williams was having with his fellow English. For that reason, as well as for others, it is unequivocally a work of genius, and it is 'ultimately national'. It is 'national music', despite the wide range of influences that can be detected within it.

The extreme reaction the Sixth provoked was the mirror-image of that caused by its predecessor. In 1943, according to the critics, Vaughan Williams had settled on the celestial city;

now the very harshness and bleakness of the Sixth seemed to portend no sort of future at all, apart from a violent and desolate one. After the mood-swings of the first movement, a tone of brutality and relentlessness, unleavened by any glimmer of sunlight, sets in for the next two: and the finale is an unrelieved pianissimo that caused some listeners to suggest, to the composer's intense disapproval, that it depicted the devastation in the aftermath of a nuclear holocaust. Vaughan Williams disliked the imputation of programmes to those of his works that had none; and he was especially sensitive about it in this case. The assumption was that this was about war, or rather the specific war that had just ended. He rejected this, though unconvincingly, quoting instead in a letter to Mr Kennedy Shakespeare's words from *The Tempest*, 'We are such stuff/As dreams are made on; and our little life/ Is rounded with a sleep.' That may well be appropriate to the ethereal ending of the work, but it hardly does for the rest of the symphony, whose inevitable images are rather those of invading armies, the blackout, Blitzkrieg and mortal combat.

Whatever inspired him was clearly intensely personal – and it seems more intensely personal, or at least more visceral, than the inspiration of perhaps any of his other works. His widow noted that 'rightly or wrongly, he never allowed the idea that lay behind the last movement of this symphony to be known'. Malcolm Sargent, who took the symphony around the world in the years immediately after its first performance, believed he knew the specific event that had prompted the work: the bomb that fell on the Café de Paris in London's west end in March 1941, killing the bandleader Ken 'Snakehips' Johnson and some of his West Indian Dance Orchestra, as well as many of the *habitués* of the Café. Certainly, the way the jazz saxophone in the scherzo is first brutalised and then snuffed out, to be supplanted by the eerie finale, suggests something more than just a Shakespearean vision.

The following year, after a notice in *The Times* of a Proms performance of the Sixth called it 'The war symphony', Vaughan Williams wrote to Frank Howes, the paper's chief music critic, to tell him: 'I dislike that implied connection very much. Of course there is nothing to prevent any writer from expressing his opinion to that effect in a notice, but it is quite a different thing, this reference to a supposed title, as if it were official on my part.' To another correspondent, he complained: 'It never seems to occur to people that a man might just want to write a piece of music.' The description of it he liked best was Rutland Boughton's: 'an agnostic's Paradiso'. What remains beyond doubt is that the Sixth's début was not just a turning-point in its composer's, and Britain's, musical life; it was, and remains, an event in the front rank of British cultural history.

Vaughan Williams's widow, on hearing that first performance, was left 'cold and frightened' by it: even though she had heard the earlier rehearsals. Deryck Cooke reflected that 'as a work of art it more than deserved the overwhelming applause it got, but I was no more able to applaud than at the end of Tchaikovsky's *Pathétique* Symphony – less so, in fact, for this seemed to be an ultimate nihilism beyond Tchaikovsky's conceiving: every drop of blood seemed frozen in one's veins.' Another critic, Hugh Ottaway, found it 'a quite shattering experience', which mirrored the sensation felt by Müller-Hartmann at the first orchestral play-through.

The audience who heard it then, and those who heard it at the hundred or so performances it had in the following two years – in the English canon only Elgar's First Symphony had received greater attention – took to it because they, having lived through the war like the composer, understood its language and its meaning, which did not have to be explained to be comprehensible. Sargent, who by this time had had a quarter-century-long association with Vaughan Williams, and who was passionate about his music, seems to have been a perfect representative of the popular view of the symphony. Taking it to Buenos Aires in 1950, he termed it 'a frightening symphony . . . the complete testament of a man who, in his seventies, looks back on the human sufferings of his time. I never conduct the Sixth without feeling that I am walking across bomb sites . . . Chaos, despair, desolation and the peace that flows from desolation.' When a local doubted whether the people of Buenos Aires, not having experienced the late war, would be able to comprehend all this, Sargent told him: 'A city which can't understand the Sixth Symphony of Vaughan Williams deserves to be bombed.'

SEVEN

To Be a Pilgrim

As we have seen, it had been imagined when he wrote his Fifth Symphony that Vaughan Williams, then over seventy, was signalling a serene end to his career and the start of twilight. Not the least remarkable of the effects the Sixth had was to force a revision not just of that assumption, but of any received idea of where the composer's creative instincts were leading him. In the years that remained to him there would be three more symphonies and several significant minor works; and all the time Vaughan Williams was acting as a living, breathing figurehead at the front of a national musical life that had rarely been so rich – including as it did Bax, Britten, Walton, Tippett, Bliss, Howells and, less celebrated but still producing works that would last, the likes of Finzi, Moeran and the young George Lloyd.

Working on his music for the Scott film in the spring and summer of 1948, Vaughan Williams began to feel it could be transformed into a symphony. It was not, however, his first priority; his seemingly endless task of trying to make an opera (or, as he now preferred to term it, a morality) out of *The Pilgrim's Progress* was, he felt, nearing its end. Ever since 1944 he had been working at the morality quite intensely; and in early December 1948 he arranged a play-through of the material at the Arts Council, at which, rather charmingly, he sang all the parts himself.

The reaction among the limited audience depressed him: he told his wife that those who heard it were 'coldly polite'. It was something of a come-down after all the years of effort, the recent heightened expectation, and the acclaim the composer had enjoyed so recently because of his spectacular new symphony. He did not have the best of health that winter; he was so dogged by a persistent cold and cough, and increasing pains in his ankles for the alleviation of which he was advised to lose weight, that he realised he would, at last, have to scale down what he was used to doing. Some things were essential, such as his presence at the recording sessions in February 1949 at which Boult was committing the Sixth Symphony to disc. His activities in conducting choirs, usually in the Bach Passions, had to be reduced. Yet, in his composing, he once more connected with musicians at the grass roots, accepting a commission from the Rural Music Schools to write a *Concerto Grosso* that contained parts for all levels of expertise. He also began working on a setting of a poem that he had once considered making into an opera, Matthew Arnold's *The Scholar Gypsy*, which he decided to use with a small orchestra and a speaker. The work became *An Oxford Elegy*, and was ready for a private run-through at his home in December 1949.

Despite the earlier depression that had set in about *The Pilgrim's Progress* he persisted throughout 1950 with trying to arrange a professional performance of the work; he had not come so far, after so long, only to be frustrated when the end was in sight. He was still gripped by Bunyan's story; in an angry letter to his fellow composer Rutland Boughton, explaining why he had refused to sign a 'peace pledge' inspired by the Soviet Union, he said that even the Russians had now admitted that the document 'was designed to weaken the resistance to their nefarious designs of tyranny and imperialistic aggression'. He told Boughton, who signed up to this doctrine wholeheartedly, that 'some of your ideas are a good deal more moribund than Bunyan's theology: – the old fashioned republicanism and Marxism which led direct to the appalling dictatorships of Hitler, Stalin and Mussolini, or your Rationalism, which dates from about 1880 and has entirely failed to solve any problems of the Universe'. Vaughan Williams was, despite the tenor of some of his music, neither a reactionary nor a nostalgic – something else that marked him out from Elgar. He never minded the modern world, or felt himself a Victorian clinging on to a golden past; but he was equally determined that the future would not repeat the mistakes of the recent past in some illusory pursuit of a 'new order'.

Although his music had for some years been aggressively contemporary in its inspiration, by clinging to Bunyan, Vaughan Williams was seeking to preserve some very old English values. He appears to have been doing this not to pretend that the awfulness of the modern world had not happened, but by way of advocating a means to temper it. In political terms, his dilute socialism was now fully confirmed as federalism; since before the war he had believed that only a federation of the world could provide the necessary unity to avoid such conflagrations. His nationalism had only ever been cultural; and if there was a contradiction between espousing cultural nationalism, and not expecting the national identity it would create to conflict with the ideals of federalism, he did not seem to see it.

His wife was by this time incredibly frail, spiritually as well as physically, and this began to take a toll on him. When he conducted the Sixth Symphony at the Three Choirs in September 1950 it exhausted him so much that he resolved never to try to conduct it again. Work ground to a halt on the symphony he was trying to forge out of the *Scott* music, which he now knew as *Sinfonia Antartica*. Robert Müller-Hartmann, with whom he had come into the habit of discussing work in progress – something he felt unable to do with almost anyone else apart from his wife – died suddenly just before Christmas 1950, a blow that affected him professionally as well as personally. Yet despite this adversity the creative spark had not been snuffed out, and never would be so long as he lived. He started work on a new cantata, *The Sons of Light*, but by early 1951, with performances of *The Pilgrim's Progress* at last scheduled for Covent Garden in April as part of the opera house's contribution to the Festival of Britain, more and more of his time and energy were occupied with travelling to London for rehearsals and discussions about the staging. At the same time *Hugh the Drover* was revived at Sadler's Wells, which improved his morale about a part of his work that meant much to him but had been downgraded and disregarded by even the most favourable of his critics.

He was usually tense before a first performance of one of his works, but the time leading up to the *Pilgrim*'s first performance was especially trying for him. The stresses he felt at witnessing, for good or bad, the realisation of what was effectively a life-long project finally overcame him as he went to his seat in the opera house on that first night, when he 'blazed with rage', in the words of his widow, at a hapless photographer who, quite understandably, sought to take his picture. Although he took a curtain call, he was under no illusions about what everyone had thought of this strange realisation of his very personal vision. He told Ursula Wood after the event that 'they won't like it, they don't want an opera with no heroine and no love duets – and I don't care, it's what I meant, and there it is'. The critics, like the first audience at the play-through, were 'coldly polite'. Perhaps they had hoped that the first major work since the Sixth would continue the remarkable artistic progress of the composer; but it did not and, if anything, seemed to take several steps back. The Sixth had greatly enhanced Vaughan Williams's reputation; the *Pilgrim* now appeared to put matters into reverse.

The music itself is consistently intense and beautiful. Having been written over so long a span of the composer's career, there are inevitably echoes of earlier music and phases in that career. Allusions to the *Tallis Fantasia*, the Fifth Symphony and even the occasional echo of the Sixth are obvious; music from the 1943 broadcast, and virtually all the *Delectable Mountains* episode, are included. Yet one senses the piece of Vaughan Williams's to which this morality owes the most is *Sancta Civitas*, whose tone of austere beauty permeates the whole work, and which, coming after the Sixth Symphony, causes the *Pilgrim* to sound occasionally anachronistic. If the audience then were left a little cold by it, that seems to have been on account of the staging and not because of the music or its libretto, which the composer had adapted mainly from Bunyan. The composer was angered by suggestions that it should be staged in a cathedral rather than in an opera house, but to an extent he had already contradicted himself by denying it the name of 'opera' in favour of 'morality'.

The *Daily Telegraph*'s critic said that the production was 'so wanting in the dramatic element – so anti-theatrical'. It certainly would have benefited from not having to meet the conventional expectations of opera, and instead to have taken its place as a latter-day *Gerontius*. This, however, the composer was beyond seeing, which can scarcely be surprising after the amount of his life that he had devoted to the project. Returning to his theme later the same week, the *Telegraph* critic argued, cogently, that the work was an 'aftermath', and that in the symphonies – the previous three in particular – the emotions that should have been expressed and realised by the *Pilgrim* had already been worked through; perhaps if Vaughan Williams had stirred himself to complete it earlier, its reception would have been better and its reputation more secure. However, by the time it was unveiled, his own art had already moved on past it. Lunching a year or two afterwards with Michael Kennedy, who admired the work, Vaughan Williams simply said: 'The Pilgrim's dead, and that's that,' in, Mr Kennedy notes, 'a manner which allowed of no contradiction and manifestly concealed a bitter disappointment'.

When the work was broadcast by the BBC on 30 April

1951 Vaughan Williams felt the performance was better, but by that time he had another, even more painful, concern. His wife, who had wanted so much to hear the wireless broadcast, had been too ill to do even that. She was now confined to bed. It was clear her frame could not support her for much longer. By 10 May she had seemed better, so much so that he felt able to leave her to come to London for a rehearsal by a student choir of *Toward the Unknown Region*. While it was taking place, she died.

Her death was hardly unexpected, and it seems to have been something of a liberation for her widower. He immediately asked Ursula Wood, who had been virtually a member of the household ever since the death of her husband, to manage his domestic affairs for him, and to spend half her week with him. He cleared up Adeline's effects and threw himself into the necessary administration caused by her death. He cancelled no engagements but strove, at the age of seventy-eight, to get on with the rest of his life without retrospection or regret. Inevitably, as his widow recalls, there were moments when the enormity of the loss of his wife of fifty-three years caught up with him: he wrote to friends, 'My wife died about a month ago, so now I am all alone'. Yet, ironically, his bereavement brought him a new lease of life, recreational as well as creative. He was no longer tied to his home as he had been throughout the years of Adeline's illness, and could contemplate travelling again, and spending more time in London, which he had missed since moving to the country.

In terms of work, he set about making improvements to *The Pilgrim's Progress*, once again demonstrating his belief that a musical composition is never really 'finished'. It went on tour later that year, and *Sir John in Love* was put on at the Royal Academy of Music and in Birmingham, where he attended performances after hearing his Fifth Symphony and *Sancta Civitas* at the Three Choirs. He was at last getting his *Scott* music into a final symphonic shape, though with the help of a young musician, Roy Douglas. Vaughan Williams's handwriting had by now deteriorated almost to illegibility, and Müller-Hartmann was no longer there to help him 'wash' his scores. Errors on a manuscript could have unfortunate results, and Douglas's job was to clean up what the composer had done, as Müller-Hartmann had occasionally done before him.

For intellectual refreshment, Vaughan Williams and Ursula Wood set about re-reading the whole Shakespeare canon, which took them a year. He had always read voraciously, not least in the search of inspiration for his music; and it was a recreation in which he became more energetic with the years. At the end of 1951 Winston Churchill, as Chancellor of the University of Bristol, presented him with the university's first honorary doctorate of music, praising him as 'our greatest English composer, and great musical ambassador'.

The spring of 1952 was spent largely getting *Sinfonia Antartica* to the point where it could be shown to John Barbirolli, who was to have the first performance. Barbirolli had just given a complete cycle of the other six symphonies with the Hallé, and Vaughan Williams had been so impressed both by the interpretations and by the personality of the conductor that he thought him and his orchestra the ideal recipients of the new work. Roy Douglas played it through at the Oxford University Press, Vaughan Williams's publishers, in March, with a select audience that included Gerald Finzi and Arthur Bliss. That same month he conducted two performances of *A Sea Symphony* with the Hallé, one in Manchester and the other in Sheffield, where one of the Hallé's cellists was too ill to play, and Barbirolli took his place. At the Manchester concert he renewed his friendship with Michael Kennedy, a devoted admirer who had for some years been a regular correspondent and who had earlier made a pilgrimage to The White Gates. He would become a close friend and also write the definitive book on Vaughan Williams's music. Mr Kennedy, who at twenty-five was fifty-four years' Vaughan Williams's junior, found him 'immensely young at heart and in mind – I never felt he was an old man . . . he believed the future belonged to the young (not "yoof") and did all he could to help and encourage them'. He also noted that the composer 'was much less austere as a man than some of the music suggests': a paradox common to many artists. He discovered in the composer a sense of humour that could be 'Rabelaisian', and when he laughed 'his whole body shook in abandoned enjoyment'.

Having not been abroad since before the war, and never having flown, Vaughan Williams went to France with Ursula Wood for a holiday that spring. After Paris and Chartres they visited Saint-Malo and the Mont Saint-Michel, where he had last been seventy years earlier as a boy of ten with his family. On his return he began to sit to Sir Gerald Kelly for a portrait commissioned by the Royal College of Music, and on 19 June his *Oxford Elegy* had its first performance in the city itself. It is another one of those works that divides the composer's admirers, its weakness being the somewhat problematic role of a speaker reciting Arnold's poetry to the backdrop of the music; to the less theatrically minded it seems somewhat arch. He went to Norfolk the following month to lecture on English folk-songs at the King's Lynn Festival, almost fifty years after he had first gone there to collect them; the Queen Mother and Princess Margaret were in his audience, and he was presented to them afterwards.

A new wave of creativity engulfed him. In another radical musical departure, he wrote a *Romance* for harmonica and orchestra, which Larry Adler performed at the Proms. Adler apparently complained about the work being impossible to play 'without a pair of auxiliary lungs', to which the composer is said to have threatened to 'rescore the whole bloody thing for bass tuba'. He was also working on revisions to the Spenser masque on which he and Ursula Wood had collaborated before the war, and which had never had a performance. As well as revising it, he set about expanding it. However, the main focus of the autumn of 1952 was his eightieth birthday celebrations. The Incorporated Society of Musicians gave a dinner in his honour, at which Herbert Howells delivered the main tribute, and there were celebration concerts both at Dorking and in London. He found it disagreeable to be the centre of attention, though he was not a man of false modesty or manufactured humility. The grandest event was a party given for him by the London County Council on the birthday itself in the Festival Hall, and a concert for which he had chosen the programme:

Thanksgiving for Victory, the Fifth Symphony, *Flos Campi* and *The Sons of Light*.

Once the celebrations were over, he made a journey to Manchester to attend rehearsals for *Sinfonia Antartica*. Its first performance was scheduled for January 1953, and on the night before travelling up to it he asked Ursula Wood to marry him. An age difference of almost forty years made no odds to either of them, and she accepted immediately. The symphony had a successful début, though it caused none of the sensation its predecessor had. Then, of course, for all its coldness and strange beauty it was in part a familiar work because of the celebrated nature of the film it had illustrated, and lacked the mystery – or mystique – that had under-pinned the creation of the Sixth. Nor can it be said to have had anything like the personal resonance with its creator that the Sixth manifestly had, or to have represented any great intellectual departure in his art. Finally, it lacked the aspect of common experience that linked composer and audience, as the Sixth had done so thoroughly. The Hallé gave a second performance the following night, and the first London per-formance was given the next week, with a broadcast a day later. Questions were raised about the work's form. Adrian Boult, one of Vaughan Williams's greatest admirers, felt that 'the *Antartica* doesn't really rank as a symphony. In fact, I would say that *Job* is really more of a symphony than the *Antartica*.'

The wedding was less of a performance. It took place quietly on 7 February, the bridegroom having asked a friend to deputise for him in rehearsing the choir at Dorking for its latest performance of the *St Matthew Passion*, though without giving the reason. Only one Sunday newspaper managed to find the story. The newlyweds made immediate plans to take a house in London, and through a friend found a vacant Crown lease on a house in Hanover Terrace, overlooking Regent's Park. Although in his eighty-first year, Vaughan Williams felt that the twenty-one-year lease was 'rather short' and asked whether it might be extended once expired. Following the success of his French trip the previous year, he and his new wife then went to Italy. They were back in time not just for the Coronation – for which Vaughan Williams had written a motet, *O Taste and See*, and had made an arrangement of *The Old One Hundredth* that all in the congregation could sing – but to attend rehearsals at Sadler's Wells for both *Riders to the Sea* and *Hugh the Drover*. In the same week as they were revived he attended the first performance of Benjamin Britten's opera to mark the new Elizabethan age, *Gloriana*. After some widespread criticism of this work, Vaughan Williams again showed his generosity towards a fellow composer, in this case one of arguably greater instinctive genius but of a very different school. He wrote to *The Times:* 'The important thing to my mind, at the moment, is that, as far as I know, for the first time in history the Sovereign has commanded an opera by a composer of these islands for a great occasion. Those who cavil at the public expense involved should realise what such a gesture means to the prestige of our own music.'

His next new work was the Christmas cantata *Hodie*, which he had worked on throughout 1953. It included settings of poems about Christmas, including verse written by his new wife. It was first played through at the RCM in September

1953, its first public performance being at the Three Choirs in September 1954. At almost an hour long it is one of his major choral works, and one which reflects the joyousness of the Christmas story: yet it also sounds anachronistic and a little self-indulgent – one critic referred to it as being 'under-composed' – and Mr Kennedy observed in the reaction to it the start of the anti-Vaughan Williams movement that would take off after his death but which, his having lived so long, appeared to have jumped the gun a little. In fact, that movement had really had its origins in the wake of *The Pilgrim's Progress*. The problem with Vaughan Williams's having had such a golden age of choral composition – from the mid-twenties to the mid-thirties, with works such as *Sancta Civitas*, *Dona Nobis Pacem* and the *Five Tudor Portraits* – is that later works sound rooted in that era and in that style; by the mid-fifties, it sounded not so much monumental as sepulchral, though that matters far less today.

Much more of a piece with his contemporary style was the concerto he wrote in 1953 for tuba and orchestra, its first performance intended for the London Symphony Orchestra's golden jubilee in June 1954. Critics considered this, too, to be a bizarre work for the composer to write: but it is so successful a concerto precisely because the composer uses it to explore the full potential of this under-regarded instrument, and couples it with some particularly sunlit orchestral writing. Much of it presages the Eighth Symphony, which was then taking shape, including some actual advance quotation: or perhaps it is the symphony that quotes from the Tuba Concerto. Although only a short work – under a quarter of an hour – it embodies great feeling, the obvious humorous capabilities of the tuba's sound being forgone in favour of its knack of creating an impression of melancholy. This is very much Vaughan Williams in his last phase, the music – especially that of the ravishing romanza – conveying perfectly the quietnesses of evening and the massive human experience of the philosopher-composer who wrote it.

In the autumn of 1953 Adrian Boult was recording the cycle of the seven symphonies for Decca with the London Philharmonic Orchestra in the Kingsway Hall, with the composer mostly present. Although his routine had moderated somewhat with the years, he still composed from 9.30 a.m. until 1 p.m. most days, with more work following his afternoon nap and stroll. His health and vigour appeared to have recovered following the long autumn in which he had been devoted to his sick wife. Now, he and Ursula devoted more time to travelling. He had never been to Rome, and went there in the spring of 1954, returning to London in time to hear Barbirolli conduct the first performance of the Tuba Concerto. He then spent much of the summer writing a programme of lectures he had been invited to give in America, at Cornell University, where he had been awarded a visiting professorship. As well as the first performance, somewhat out of season, of *Hodie* at the Three Choirs Festival that autumn, he also conducted his *Pastoral Symphony* and *Flos Campi*.

Then he and his wife went off by sea to New York, a place he had come to regard as 'the most beautiful city in the world', and thence to Cornell University at Ithaca to deliver his lectures. That done, he embarked on a wider North American lecture tour, first to Toronto, then to Buffalo and

Detroit, St Louis, then the long overland train journey to Los Angeles. Once in California the Vaughan Williamses had a week's holiday by the sea at Santa Barbara; and it was on the train journey back east that they fulfilled the dream of visiting the Grand Canyon, though the composer rejected the plan of riding by mule down to the bottom as he could find no beast he thought would take his weight. Once back in Buffalo he rehearsed the Buffalo Orchestra in *A London Symphony*, which he was to conduct as the first of several concerts with them.

At Cornell he had displayed the same eagerness he had at home to listen to new works by younger composers – he was often to be seen in the stalls of the London concert-halls at the first performances of works by Britten, Tippett and Walton, as well as concerts of works by less celebrated men. 'He disliked most modern music,' Mr Kennedy has noted, 'but always listened to it in case something was there. He got this from Parry.' He had listened patiently at Cornell while a student played him one of his own distinctly modern, lengthy compositions on the piano; after which Vaughan Williams said to him: 'Very interesting, my boy, but if a tune *should* occur to you, don't hesitate to write it down.'

Finale

The Vaughan Williamses were back home for Christmas, the two main by-products of the trip being a set of lectures prepared for publication and a well-advanced score of the Eighth Symphony. By April 1955 this work was ready for its first play-through, though it created some uncertainty among its initial audience. Frank Howes, the music critic who had just finished a book on the composer, wrote to him to cast doubt on the music's suitability to be a symphony. Vaughan Williams told him: 'I feel the thing is a symphony and it is going to remain one . . . I shall probably do nothing till I have let it "mature in bond" for a bit.' In his eventual programme note the composer answered this criticism again by saying that 'I understand that some hearers may have their withers wrung by a work being called a symphony whose first movement does not correspond to the usual symphonic form'. It was all, he continued, a matter of definition and interpretation. He wanted Barbirolli to have the first performance, and showed him the score that spring: the conductor said he was 'greatly intrigued by it'. It is the natural sibling of the Tuba Concerto; not only is there the same autumnal tone, but also the same willingness to experiment with the orchestra and with individual instruments, not gratuitously, but to hear exactly what they could do.

That might give the impression that it is an exhibition piece of some sort, rather than something stimulated by deep emotions; that that is not the case is, however, apparent immediately upon hearing the work. The first movement, played by the whole orchestra, is a fantasia of 'variations without a theme'; it is haunting, passionate, tightly structured and begins and ends with an enigma. The second movement is just for wind and brass, the third a cavatina for strings, the finale a toccata that includes 'all the 'phones and 'spiels known to the composer'. Among the percussion are three tuned gongs, the legacy of an unplanned afternoon visit to a performance of *Turandot* at Covent Garden during the symphony's composition, where Vaughan Williams heard the instruments and decided they ought to be part of the new musical exploration he was making. If this was thought to be too playful or trivial, the composer saw to it that the work ends on what he called a 'sinister' note. If it does – and it is a matter of taste, or how seriously one chooses to take him – then it drops the most accurate possible hint about the symphony that would come next.

In the summer of 1955 Vaughan Williams became the first musician ever to receive the Albert Medal of the Royal Society of Arts. His music was now constantly performed by amateurs and professionals the length and breadth of England; earlier in the year the City of Birmingham Symphony Orchestra had joined those giving the cycle of his symphonies, and most festivals seemed to feature at least one of his choral works, fulfilling his intention of writing music that the English people could make. If a backlash was starting against him, it was still confined to certain critics. He had hardly written any film music since *Scott* – paradoxically, considering the success of that enterprise – but was asked to provide a score for a short documentary, *The England of Elizabeth*. This occupied him for much of late 1955, after returning from a tour of Greece, his first time there since the expedition to Salonika during the Great War. It is grand music, conveying perfectly the adventurousness and dynamism of the Tudors and typically laced with references to the musical culture of that time.

Despite his great age, and as a further testament to his vigour, he was still conducting, mostly his own works – though he still could not handle the Sixth Symphony – and performances of the Bach Passions, which in early 1956 he did with the Hallé in Manchester as well as at Dorking. Barbirolli had no doubts that the work Vaughan Williams considered to be his Eighth Symphony was, indeed, a symphony, and the Hallé rehearsed it that winter with the composer present. Vaughan Williams, for his part, was sufficiently pregnant with inspiration that he set about sketching a ninth symphony before the Eighth had even been launched, as if he knew that only limited time remained for him. The Eighth had its début, to mixed reviews, in May 1956, the novelty of the musical forces and their arrangement causing some difficulties to the critics. The idea that this remarkable and beautiful work was in fact an essay in gimmickry and invention for the sake of invention took hold among some critics and seemed to satisfy them greatly.

The critical coolness towards the symphony may, in retrospect, have been provoked not especially by anything in the work itself. Since the success of the Sixth Symphony subsequent works had been greeted by a growing scepticism about Vaughan Williams's cultural contribution to English music. As a person he was revered, even loved: the feeling was now rampant that he had, along with the rest of the musical establishment of the first forty years of the century, led English music into some sort of cultural isolation ward, kept in quarantine from the intellectual influences of Stravinsky, Berg, Schoenberg and the rest. It was felt that English music might have travelled abroad rather better had it been able to pick up somewhat more of the so-called universal language. Vaughan Williams, despising as he did the very idea of there being such a language, was now regarded as the chief monoglot, the man whose vision of a national music rooted in folk-song had worked to choke off other influences whenever they emerged.

Much of this thought was fallacious: composers who owed nothing to the folk-song influence, such as Elgar and Britten, certainly enjoyed periods of neglect before and after their deaths, but had, and still have, huge international reputations. So, too, does Walton, whose powers as a composer tailed off in the second half of his career for reasons unconnected with the influence of Vaughan Williams on English music, an influence from which he was in any case almost totally immune. The great army of composers whom the critics of musical nationalism had hoped to enlist in a different cause might not even have had the chance to develop their talents as much as they did had

English music not found, at the end of the nineteenth century and the beginning of the twentieth, its own, confident voice with which they could agree, disagree and argue – and had it not, as a result, stimulated the interest of an audience.

Much of the early work on the Ninth Symphony was done in Majorca, where the Vaughan Williamses took their now traditional autumn holiday in 1956; while there they heard of the death of Gerald Finzi, the composer to whom Vaughan Williams had probably been closest since the death of Holst, and who after years of sickness was finally killed by chicken-pox. Vaughan Williams had always been a great encourager of musical talent in others, and that year took further practical steps to see that his good work for them could live on after him. The RVW Trust was inaugurated in November 1956, to divert all the income from his performing rights – which by then had become substantial – to enable performances of music by composers other than himself. The first project in which the Trust became engaged was to subsidise a concert of lesser-known works by Holst, something that had long been Vaughan Williams's ambition. That took place at the Festival Hall, under Boult; but the Trust would allow similar subventions to local musical societies and festivals in the interests of promoting 'national music'. Although the Holst concert was half-empty – or half-full, depending on your point of view – it ended the period of critical neglect that had prevailed since Holst's death twenty-two years earlier, and put some of his music back on the map, where it has stayed. In the sixties and seventies especially many works by lesser-known English composers were brought before the public only because the Trust subsidised recordings of them.

Vaughan Williams's iron constitution started to show signs of buckling. An attack of phlebitis shortly before his eighty-fourth birthday caused him to cancel an appearance at the Cheltenham Festival; though when Michael Kennedy asked him whether there was any message he could relay to his admirers there, the composer told him: 'Yes, tell them there's no need to enquire about me in hushed tones.' Early in 1957, with the Ninth Symphony now well advanced, he was felled by anaemia after an early summer holiday in Austria and Bavaria – on which he heard, in the distance, the sound of a flugelhorn, which he duly incorporated into his new symphony. After feeling ill for several weeks that summer with a recurrence of his phlebitis, he was taken into hospital for tests and X-rays. A non-malignant tumour was discovered in his prostate. As a result he had to return to hospital at the end of the summer for a major operation, from which he recovered surprisingly quickly. He went to Mrs Finzi's house at Ashmansworth in Berkshire to convalesce, where he set about completing the Ninth Symphony.

His Eighth was given at the Last Night of the Proms, for which its exuberance made it a natural fit, and the first performance of *Epithalamion*, the choral version of *The Bridal Day*, at last took place on 30 September. The masque was a charming throwback to its time, the late thirties, and sounds a companion piece to the *Five Tudor Portraits*; it would not have appealed in 1957, though its virtues are quite audible now and redolent of the genteel amateur music-making of the provincial festivals for which the composer was unashamed to write. He was well enough to be present at the first performance and, at the time of his eighty-fifth birthday in October, to attend the celebration concert given by the Royal Philharmonic Society, for which he chose the programme: the *Pastoral Symphony*, *On Wenlock Edge* in the orchestral version, and *Job*. Dorking gave a party for him a couple of days later, where at his request there was no music but, instead, a performance by a conjuror. On the birthday itself he was inundated with congratulations, as befitted one of the greatest living Englishmen of the time, and a towering figure in the nation's culture.

Once the festivities were over, he set about finishing the new symphony with the usual assistance afterwards from Roy Douglas. In November 1957 the first play-through took place at the London flat of the man who would conduct it on its début, Malcolm Sargent, the select audience including Arthur Bliss and Herbert Howells. Although phlebitis again meant that for several days on end Vaughan Williams had to be confined to bed, it did not still his creativity. In a few days late in 1957 he wrote *Ten Blake Songs*, which he set for tenor and oboe, in response to a commission from makers of a short film marking the poet's bicentenary. His physical faculties were soon improved to match his intellectual ones: he was able to conduct the *St John Passion* at Dorking in February 1958, though it took a great deal out of him, and his health once more deteriorated. The normal apprehension he felt before the performance of a major new work also began to get to him, as the Ninth Symphony was to have its first performance in April. When it came, the reception – as much for composer as work, with the audience giving him a standing ovation as he entered the hall – was enthusiastic, though the symphony was so different from its predecessor, and so reflective and dark, that many were unsure what to make of it.

It can now be seen as not just the most powerful musical expression the composer had made since the Sixth Symphony – with which it shares the key of E minor – but as one of the most powerful he ever made. It is the consummation of that theme of melancholy, derived from folk-song but much developed, that echoes throughout so much of the composer's output: what Matthew Arnold, a century earlier, had called 'the eternal note of sadness'. The opening movement is stern and expansive, lacking the ferocity and pace of the beginning of the Sixth but creating instead an overwhelming impression of sombreness and reflectiveness unrelieved, unlike in the Sixth, by the impertinences of jazz-rhythms. As in the Eighth, there is a sense of evening; but this is a gloomier end of day, with few shafts of late sunlight. The second movement opens with the mournful flugelhorn, itself soon trumped by heavy, dark chords from the brass, though these are in time relieved by a more stately, though mournful, passage for strings and woodwind, which the composer termed a 'romantic episode'. There is again a sense of expansiveness, consistent with the original programme the composer had for the work: that it was a Hardyesque conception inspired by, and seeking to reflect, the area of Salisbury Plain and Stonehenge, with its vast uninterrupted landscape and its ancient, atavistic connections. A scherzo that is also a close relative of the Sixth Symphony, with saxophones, an insolent march tune and a flavour of jazz, precedes a wistful, ever darker finale, whose relentlessness becomes majestic, and provides one of the few 'big endings' in Vaughan Williams's music; the very end is like, to quote Whitman as set in *A Sea Symphony*, 'Waves spreading far as the eye can see', though it is more likely to reflect the fate of Tess of the d'Urbervilles, after the police have finally found her at Stonehenge. It is a deeply troubling work, not for any intellectual or technical problems it raises, but because of what it reveals about the composer's soul and his preparation to confront mortality. Mr Kennedy has said of Vaughan Williams: 'I think he remained an optimist about mankind and the human spirit, although I'm never quite sure what the end of the Ninth is telling us in that respect.' It may be that optimism for the living world is balanced by the old atheist's pessimism about the oblivion that comes with the grave.

It is not just because we know now how shortly this work preceded Vaughan Williams's death that it is one of his works that provides the most emotional experience to the listener. It is a deeply human piece of music, though not just about man but about nature; it embodies all the pain of the experience of the twentieth century, but also much that is timeless about England and the English landscape, without ever once being clichéd or predictable. It is a masterpiece not just of emotion, but of invention: yet it suffered, like its predecessor, from critical disdain. In that, it was even more the victim of the prevailing climate of musical opinion than the Eighth was; yet it is not remotely a backward-looking work, it is in many ways the most progressive, original music the composer had ever written. It now enjoys so high a reputation because its language is once more appreciated, and it is seen to be of a piece with its predecessors both in terms of its beauty and its message. It suffered at the time of its first performance, too, from under-rehearsal, and it had only as much as it did because the composer had been prepared to pay handsomely for it. The critical reception reached new depths of hostility, with some accusing Vaughan Williams of writing music for the sake of it, of being technically naive, and the second movement even being branded as 'silly' and 'asinine'. The composer's response to such abuse was to reflect that 'I don't think they can quite forgive me for still being able to do it at my age.' As Mr Kennedy noted: 'He knew the tide had turned.'

Vaughan Williams and his wife went abroad, first to Naples and then to Ischia to stay with the William Waltons, by way of recuperation. There was still no intention of giving up; he wanted to write another opera, with a libretto by his wife, and their thoughts turned to this on Ischia, the subject being a mélange of two ballads, *Thomas the Rhymer* and *Tam Lin*. Also, in keeping with his view that a piece of music is never finished, he set about revising the score of his new symphony.

Once back home, in June 1958, Vaughan Williams was seized with an urge to travel around England. The first excursion was to Lincolnshire, including a visit to his cousin Diana Montgomery-Massingberd at Gunby, and one to Cambridge. He then attended the Cheltenham Festival, taking every opportunity to get out into the Gloucestershire countryside. He threw himself into a campaign – becoming its vice-president – to save the Third Programme from threatened BBC cuts. In high summer there was a short

London season of *Sir John in Love*, which pleased a composer whose operatic efforts meant more to him than most people realised; and in early August the new symphony was performed at the Proms, with a recording by Boult scheduled for the end of the month. If the tide had turned once, there was always the chance that it would turn again. After that Proms performance a critic who had rarely been sympathetic to his music, Neville Cardus, wrote that,

> Vaughan Williams's great achievement has been to dispense with the current musical coin of the period of his basic culture and maturity and to modulate to the contemporary tone and language without obvious iconoclasms . . . at the end of a strong, convincing interpretation of the Ninth Symphony by the BBC Orchestra and Sir Malcolm [Sargent], the composer walked down a high stairway, bent precariously on his stick, as he made his way to the platform to acknowledge the tumultuous applause – applause led by young people standing in the arena. It was a very moving sight; and somehow it epitomised all that we had just been hearing from the symphony.

Vaughan Williams had completed the first piano score of the new opera, and having done so went away with his wife to Dorset for a short holiday. On returning to London he discussed with his publisher the new, revised edition of *Hugh the Drover*, on which he had worked along with the symphony the previous winter. He went to bed on the evening of 25 August 1958, contemplating the recording session for his Ninth Symphony that he would attend the following day; but he died before dawn.

He had kept the faith. In one of his last public utterances, shortly before his death, he had said: 'Bach was behind the times, Beethoven was ahead of them, and yet both were the greatest of composers. Modernism and conservation are irrelevant. What matters is to be true to oneself.'

Coda

It is a tradition, at least with English composers, that a period of posthumous neglect sets in some time before rigor mortis, and indeed often before the body is dead. Elgar and Holst endured this before Vaughan Williams. Parry had an especially bad case, being routinely vilified by critics and teachers of music for the best part of seventy years after his death, before a proper reassessment and revival came in the 1980s and 1990s. By comparison, Vaughan Williams got off lightly. There was a period of quietness for four or five years: but then the appearance of his widow's biography, and Michael Kennedy's book on the music, in 1964 prompted a steady increase in interest. By the time of the centenary in 1972 Boult had undertaken another cycle of the symphonies, and André Previn had recorded his own. The centenary itself had a high profile; all nine symphonies were performed at the Proms, there was a special centenary concert on 12 October, the BBC broadcast many of these performances, and the Post Office issued a commemorative stamp.

From then on the popularity of the composer, as marked by recordings of his works and public performances, continued to grow. Perhaps it was that his lack of association with the unfashionable parts of Britain's recent past, notably imperialism and reactionary politics, meant there were not the intellectual barriers between his music and a supposedly radical younger generation that Elgar, for example, seemed to provoke. In so far as Vaughan Williams's music had a programme, it was one entirely relevant to the late twentieth century: peace, natural beauty, the meaning of existence, the uncertainty of our spiritual life.

However, at over forty years' remove from the man himself, the work can be seen in its proper perspective; and appreciated, as it should principally be, for its sheer beauty and aesthetic force rather than for any 'programme' or lack of it. If in that beauty and force there are atavistic qualities that cause English listeners, at least, to feel a connection with an instinctual past and a common heritage, that is no more than the composer himself would have wanted.

Bibliography

Barlow, Michael, *Whom the Gods Love: the Life and Music of George Butterworth* (Toccata Press, 1997)

Boult, Sir Adrian, *Boult on Music* (Toccata Press, 1983)

Cooke, Deryck, *The Language of Music* (OUP, 1959)

Dibble, Jeremy, *C. Hubert H. Parry: His Life and Music* (OUP, 1992)

Foreman, Lewis (ed.), *From Parry to Britten: British Music in Letters 1900–1945* (Batsford, 1987)

Kennedy, Michael, *Adrian Boult* (Hamish Hamilton, 1987)

—, *Portrait of Walton* (OUP, 1989)

—, *The Works of Ralph Vaughan Williams* (Clarendon Press, Second Edition, 1992)

—, *A Catalogue of the Works of Ralph Vaughan Williams* (OUP, Second Edition, 1996)

Lees-Milne, James, *Prophesying Peace* (Chatto and Windus, 1977)

Mellers, Wilfrid, *Vaughan Williams and the Vision of Albion* (Barrie and Jenkins, 1989)

Montgomery-Massingberd, John, *Happy Days at Gunby: A Musical Memorial* (The National Trust, 1996)

Ottaway, Hugh, *Vaughan Williams Symphonies* (BBC Publications, 1972)

Reid, Charles, *Malcolm Sargent* (Hamish Hamilton, 1968)

Short, Michael, *Gustav Holst: The Man and his Music* (OUP, 1990)

Stradling, Robert, and Hughes, Meirion, *The English Musical Renaissance 1860–1940* (Routledge, 1993)

Trend, Michael, *The Music Makers* (Schirmer, 1985)

Vaughan Williams, Ralph, *National Music and other essays* (OUP, Second Edition, 1987)

Vaughan Williams, Ralph and Holst, Gustav, *Heirs and Rebels: Letters written to each other and occasional writings on music*, (OUP, 1959)

Vaughan Williams, Ursula, *RVW: A Biography of Ralph Vaughan Williams* (OUP, 1964)

Select Discography

Vaughan Williams's music has been extensively recorded, particularly since the boom in his popularity in the mid-eighties. Almost every piece of music he published is now available on compact disc: a notable exception is the operetta *The Poisoned Kiss*. Cycles of the symphonies have been, or are being, recorded by Sir Adrian Boult, André Previn, Vernon Handley, Bernard Haitink, Leonard Slatkin, Kees Bakels, Bryden Thomson, Sir Roger Norrington and Sir Andrew Davis. In my opinion, the best recent cycle is Slatkin's (RCA Victor Red Seal). Other notable recordings are Boult's 1953 account of the *Sea Symphony*, with soloists Dame Isobel Baillie and John Cameron (Belart 450 144–2), the composer's own recording of the F Minor (No. 4) of 1937 (coupled with Barbirolli's 1944 recording of the Fifth), (Avid AMSC 599), and a live performance of the Sixth by Barbirolli, made shortly before his death, with the Symphonieorchester des Bayerischen Rundfunks (Orfeo C 265 921 B).

The operas are all available on EMI Classics: *Hugh the Drover* conducted by Sir Charles Groves, with Robert Tear as Hugh (CMS 5 65224 2), *Sir John in Love* conducted by Meredith Davies (CMS 5 66123 2), *Riders to the Sea* conducted by Meredith Davies

(CDM 7 64730 2) and *The Pilgrim's Progress* conducted by Boult, with John Noble as the Pilgrim (CMS 7 64212 2). Of the choral music, the 1993 recording by Richard Hickox and the LSO of *Sancta Civitas* and *Dona Nobis Pacem*, with Bryn Terfel, Philip Langridge and Yvonne Kenny stands as one of the greatest recordings ever made of Vaughan Williams's music (EMI CDC 7 54788 2). Also notable is Sir David Willcocks's recording of *Five Tudor Portraits*, with Elizabeth Bainbridge and John Carol Case (EMI CDM 7 64722 2). The Christ Church Cathedral Choir's recording of the *Mass in G Minor*, directed by Stephen Darlington, is first rate (Nimbus NI 5083). Two of the best vocal recordings are Philip Langridge's *On Wenlock Edge*, with Howard Shelley (piano) and the Britten quartet, on a disc that also contains a fine account of the String Quartet in G minor of 1908 (EMI CDC 7 54346 2), and Benjamin Luxon's 1986 collection for Chandos (CHAN 8475) that includes the *Songs of Travel, Linden Lea, The House of Life* and *Four Poems by Fredegond Shove*, with David Willison (piano).

Finally, three orchestral and instrumental recordings of the highest quality: Barbirolli's legendary recording of the *Tallis Fantasia*, unsurpassed after thirty-five years (EMI CDC 7 47537 2), Vernon Handley's 1983 recording of *Job* with the London Philharmonic (CFP 7 67538 2), and the same conductor's 1984 recording of the Piano Concerto in C with Howard Shelley and the RPO (Lyrita SRCD 211), which is little short of miraculous.

Index

Blake, William, 72, 141

Blest Pair of Sirens (Parry), 8–9

Bliss, Arthur, 26, 49, 51, 73, 85, 120, 128, 141

Bloomsbury Square (London), 43

The Bold Young Sailor (folk-song), 30

Borodin, Alexander, 33

Boughton, Rutland, 118, 122

Boult, Sir Adrian, 52; and Holst, 13–14, 50, 63, 139; musical assistance to Vaughan Williams from, 38–39; on Vaughan Williams, 111–12, 130; as Vaughan Williams's champion, 60; Vaughan Williams's works conducted by, 55–56, 76, 84, 85, 98, 108, 110, 121, 133, 145, 147

Bournemouth (England), 22, 27

Brahms, Johannes, 5, 9, 33, 40

Brentwood (Essex), 23

The Bridal Day (Vaughan Williams), 96, 97, 140

Bright, John, 91

Bristol (England), 98, 127

British Broadcasting Company. *See* BBC

British Museum (London), 20

British National Opera Company (BNOC), 60

Britten, Benjamin, 54, 65, 85, 115, 131; neglect of, after death, 138; on Vaughan Williams, 41; as Vaughan Wil-

liams's successor, 5, 69, 90, 134

Brooke, Rupert, 11

Brown, Haig, 7

Bruch, Max, 19

Bryn Mawr College, 76, 84

Buenos Aires (Argentina), 119

Buffalo (New York), 133–34

Buffalo Orchestra, 134

Bunyan, John, 37, 54, 91, 93, 101, 104, 107, 120–26

Bushes and Briars (folk song), 23, 25

Busoni, Ferruccio, 75

Butterworth, George, 24, 105; death of, in World War I, 42, 48, 52, 82; as leader of new generation of English national composers, 39–40, 112; on Vaughan Williams, 44, 45

Byrd, William, 8, 10

Café de Paris (London), 117–18

Cambridge (England), 144. *See also* Cambridge University

Cambridge University, 10–13, 18, 20, 36

Canada, 133

The Captain's Apprentice (folk-song), 30

Cardus, Neville, 145

Carnegie Hall (New York City), 98

Cavatina (Raff), 6

Cello Concerto (Elgar), 51

Central Office of Information, 112